NO COWARD SOLDIERS

The Nathan I. Huggins Lectures

NO COWARD SOLDIERS

Black Cultural Politics and Postwar America

Waldo E. Martin Jr.

Harvard University Press
Cambridge, Massachusetts
London, England
2005

Library of Congress Cataloging-in-Publication Data

Martin, Waldo E., 1951–
No coward soldiers : Black cultural politics and
postwar America / Waldo E. Martin, Jr.
p. cm.—(The Nathan I. Huggins lectures)
Includes bibliographical references and index.
ISBN 0-674-01507-X (alk. paper)
1. African Americans—Politics and government—20th century.
2. African Americans—Race identity. 3. African American arts—
History—20th century. 4. Politics and culture—United States—
History—20th century. I. Title. II. Series.

E185.6.M3625 2005
305.896′073′09045—dc22
2004051131

For my daughters

Jetta Grace Martin and Coral Rose Martin

Contents

List of Illustrations ix

Acknowledgments xi

Introduction: "Keep on Pushin'"
1

1. "I, Too, Sing America"
Black Cultural Politics and the National Question
10

2. "Spirit in the Dark"
Black Music and Black Freedom
44

3. "Be Real Black for Me"
Embodying and Representing Blackness
82

Epilogue: Black to the Future
132

Notes 141

Credits 153

Index 155

Illustrations

1. Jacob Lawrence, *The Ordeal of Alice*, 1963   101

2. Romare Bearden, *Conjur Woman*, 1964   104

3. Romare Bearden, *Show Time*, 1974   106

4. Elizabeth Catlett, *Homage to My Young Black Sisters*, 1968   111

5. Elizabeth Catlett, *Black Is Beautiful*, 1970   113

6. Betye Saar, *The Liberation of Aunt Jemima*, 1972   118

7. Sister Gertrude Morgan, *The Book of Revelation*, ca. 1965–1970   120

8. Gordon Parks, "Mrs. Ella Watson, Government Charwoman," 1942   124

9. Gordon Parks, "Mrs. Ella Watson with Three Grandchildren and Adopted Daughter," 1942   126

10. Roy DeCarava, "Mississippi Freedom Marcher," 1963   128

Acknowledgments

I must thank Dr. Henry Louis Gates Jr. and all those associated with the W. E. B. Du Bois Institute and the Department of African and Afro-American Studies at Harvard, as well as the active audiences there, for making the experience of giving the Nathan I. Huggins Lectures memorable. Careful critiques by Leon Litwack, Lawrence Levine, Raymond Gavins, Patricia Sullivan, Sterling Stuckey, Felicia Angeja, Ronald G. Walters, Jessica Dallow, and Douglas McAdam were crucial to my revisions of the lectures for publication. Hearty thanks go to the Identity Reading Group at the Center for Advanced Study in the Behavioral Sciences (CASBS) in 2002–03—Jane Burbank, Fred Cooper, Peter Gourevitch, Michele Lamont, Deborah Post, Alan Ryan, Stephanie Shaw, and Andrew Shyrock—for making the seminar on these lectures likewise useful for my revisions. At Harvard University Press, the keen editorial guidance of Kathleen McDermott, Ann Hawthorne, and Camille Smith enhanced the narrative and facilitated the book's production. William Wagner, my research assistant, has been invaluable in readying these essays for publication. For any errors that persist, I alone am responsible.

I want to thank both the University of California at Berkeley for the yearlong sabbatical assistance and CASBS for the yearlong fellowship. Both also helped to make this project possible. I am also grateful for the support provided for my tenure at CASBS through a grant from the Andrew W. Mellon Foundation. Likewise appreciated was a grant from Berkeley's History Department that helped defray copyright and permissions costs.

Finally, to Catherine, Jetta, and Coral—my family—I offer the deepest thanks. Their unstinting love and assistance helped to make the project not only possible, but also worthwhile.

What is most remarkable about much that is called black culture is its Americanness; and conversely, much of what is considered most uniquely American is essentially Afro-American.

NATHAN I. HUGGINS

"Keep on Pushin'"

ON FEBRUARY 1, 1960, Franklin McCain, Ezell Blair Jr., David Richmond, and Joseph McNeil—students at North Carolina Agricultural and Technical College (A&T), a black school—sat in at the lunch counter of the Woolworth's in my hometown of Greensboro, North Carolina. Even as a third-grader, I appreciated that moment's local impact. In hindsight, I also appreciate the major national significance of that hometown protest. After that heroic action, the student-led sit-in movement exploded throughout the South, further energizing the Civil Rights Movement. Subsequently a series of successful local black protests against the most egregious manifestations of Jim Crow came fast and furious.

What I remember most vividly, however, are the mass meetings, or political mobilizations, that I attended at local churches. More than the political speeches or any other aspect of these events, the freedom songs—ringing, declarative refrains like "We shall not be moved!" and "We shall overcome"—touched me and untold others most deeply. Whether rooted in secular or sacred music, the freedom songs tapped profound depths and provided cathartic healing, affirmation, and aspiration.

Those freedom songs, like the best blues, jazz, and rhythm and blues, walked the same emotional and psychological territory traversed by religious music. In his achingly slow and primal lead vocals in songs such as "Jordan River, I'm Bound to Cross," Deacon Wilkes used to work that territory on Sunday morning at United Institutional Baptist Church, my church home. Sister Ella Hampton plunged deep into that same affective space in her heart-rending and dramatic solo about heaven as a land where ultimately we will all "Never Grow Old."

In structure, pacing, spirit, and substance, then, both those mass political meetings and the Sunday worship services strike me as inseparable. The highly politicized music of the former is cut from the same cloth as many popular varieties of African-American music. Indeed, at the dynamic intersection where these various musics and rituals mimic and cross-fertilize one another, an awesome power emerges. That power is integral not only to the best of these rituals and musics, but also to the best of black expressive culture.

The politics of these musics and varieties of black expressive culture often proceed in different and at times inconsistent directions and hence are open to multiple, even conflicting, interpretations. The positions and ideologies range from radical to conservative, from the most astute political consciousness to the prepolitical and explicitly apolitical. The wide-ranging political consciousness revealed both in the musics and in the larger expressive culture are intimately connected to important individual and collective forms of black struggle, to important varieties of black cultural politics.

This book examines the way we think and write about the Civil Rights and Black Power era, what is sometimes called the Movement. More specifically, the aim is to expand and to reorient that discussion by grappling with a neglected and poorly understood theme in both scholarly and popular literature on the Movement, which is also referred to as the Black Freedom Struggle and the Black Liberation Insurgency. The vital impact of African-American culture on this transformative historical moment animates this investigation. There are already studies of the Movement's profound political, economic, and social manifestations. This book ventures in a different direction. The Civil Rights–Black Power period constitutes a profound cultural shift whose history cries out for more critical attention. Largely as a result of the increased emphasis on African-American self-definition and self-determination in this period, the emphasis on cultural struggle necessarily intensified. Cultural change was especially important to the transformative vision of the Movement. The following pages focus on how various developments, personalities, and genres in African-American culture, especially expressive culture, illuminate the relationship between the freedom struggle and black cultural politics. Precisely because African Americans historically have had more control over their own culture than many other aspects of their world, culture has always been a critical battleground in their freedom struggle.

Culture—broadly conceived as both worldview/ethos and material/class components—constitutes the stuff of lived experience and historical memory. Because these frameworks—worldview and materiality—are necessarily intertwined, "culture" in the discussion here is used to refer both to a holistic vision of life and experience and the corresponding history of that vision, and to practices and theories growing out of that history and worldview.[1]

A key concern is to assess patterns of continuity and change in black cultural politics. Principally, how do black cultural politics compare during the Civil Rights and Black Power phases of the modern African-American Liberation Insurgency? The focus here is on continuities in the context of a profound shift. This fundamental cultural shift was the embrace of black culture among blacks themselves as a critical element of the intensifying Black Freedom Struggle. As a result, varieties of black cultural politics developed that fed off of and influenced the Movement. These developments led in turn to a growing, at times ambivalent, embrace of blacks and black culture within the wider society.

By black cultural politics, I mean the inevitable politicization of culture and culturalization of politics among African Americans growing out of the imperatives of their ongoing freedom struggle. The intractable liberation struggle that Africans in America have waged since the era of slavery and slave trade down to the present has ebbed and flowed over time. In what has amounted to an enduring war, culture has been a primary battlefield.

A more precise definition of black cultural politics as employed here is in order. The operative notion of "cultural" in this case denotes "the process of mobilizing certain differences," like aesthetics and style, "and linking them to group identity."[2] Politics refers to struggles for African-American empowerment in the context of a ceaseless dual struggle. The first level of struggle is the internal world of African-American politics. The second is the complicated African-American offensive against white hegemony.

Another useful definition of black cultural politics is the intersection where culture and politics overlap and merge. Or, as Kobena Mercer has written, cultural politics are networks, or frameworks, "in which 'politics' and 'culture' neither reflect each other, determine one another, nor substitute one for the other, but enter into complex relations of mutual articulation." Like James Clifford and George E. Marcus, I "assume that the poetic and the political are inseparable." In Ross Posnock's study of cosmopolitan African-American intellectuals such as Alain Locke and W. E. B. Du Bois, he observes "how richly entangled the aesthetic and the political become."[3] In cultural politics generally and in black cultural politics specifically, the boundary between the aesthetic and the political is more apparent than real.

While to a significant extent the internal world of black politics has been shaped by white hegemony and the war against it, the former has not been wholly shaped and constrained by the latter. In other words, as Ralph Ellison persuasively admonished us, black history and culture are infinitely more complex, proactive, affirmative, and internally driven than mere responses to white oppression.[4] The focus in this analysis is accordingly expansive—a wide-ranging view of black cultural politics and the Black Freedom Struggle as well as African-American history and culture.

Between the 1940s and the 1970s, largely because of the escalating Black Freedom Struggle, black Americans—ambivalence and alienation notwithstanding—began to see themselves and their world through a lens of ever-greater hope and possibility. The expanding mass movement, on one hand, and increasing black attention to autonomous group power, especially black nation building, on the other, gathered momentum. Seen another way, the modern Black Liberation Movement between 1945 and 1975 was a series of crucial civil, political, social, and economic battles.[5] In addition, and equally significant, that movement was also a series of crucial cultural struggles. In a holistic sense, it was a ubiquitous cultural war: a tumultuous contest between blacks and their antagonists to capture the American heart and soul. This fierce series of battles over the essence of the American experience—its deepest and most enduring meanings—is what this discussion is all about.

Without understating or obscuring the centrality of the political, economic, and social dimensions of the Movement, the following chapters argue that culture and cultural struggle have been, and are, central. Culture and cultural struggle constitute our primary window onto the world. They are our principal ways of imagining and realizing our world and are crucial to being and acting in the world. Viewed from this perspective, politics is both an indispensable element and a vital expression of culture.

Cultural politics thus expresses the interpenetration of the political and the cultural and denotes contests over cultural power. In the economically and racially stratified, white-dominated

United States, the culture of African-American freedom struggle has been wide-ranging and ubiquitous.[6] During the modern Black Liberation Insurgency, the inherent fusion of culture and politics became clearer and more intense as various forms of black cultural nationalism took center stage.

These forms constituted a diverse array, from the wide-ranging Black Arts Movement, with an emphasis on artistic activism in the service of mass struggle, to the Los Angeles–based US Movement of Maulana Ron Karenga, with its avant-gardist and sectarian brand of cultural activism and struggle. The short-lived Black Arts Repertory Theater, founded in 1965 by LeRoi Jones (aka Imamu Amiri Baraka), Larry Neal, and Askia Toure, epitomized the mass spirit of grassroots artistic insurgency fueling the Black Arts Movement. Baraka later recalled that at the time, "We wanted an art that would actually reflect black life and its history and legacy of resistance and struggle!" Of necessity, this meant that "we wanted a mass art." Correspondingly, this angle of vision highlighted "artists who wanted to make revolution. Revolutionary intellectuals." While the cultural nationalism of Karenga's organization, US, shared this ideological outlook, in effect US operated as a tight-knit cadre, or cell, as compared with more community-based organizations guided by a mass vision.[7] Central to these black nationalist visions are the related beliefs that an informed consciousness shapes wise political action and that cultural struggle is essential to other facets of the liberation struggle.

Speaking of the postwar Black Freedom Movement, Vincent Harding has urged scholars to examine "the powerful release of creative energy . . . so central to that era of transformation." He has insisted that like the efforts of their far more heralded compatriots in the Black Freedom Struggle, the work of these cultural warriors has also been "fundamental to the creation of a more just and democratic society." Harding concludes that "once we free ourselves from our obsession with 'civil rights' as the essential process and goal of the post-World War II freedom movement, we are able to move . . . to a direct encounter with the artists, especially the musicians, whose 'fury for liberty' is so central to an accurate sense of this period." Similarly, Edward Said has insisted, "the intervention of non-European artists and scholars cannot be dismissed or silenced." It must be understood that "these interventions are not only an integral part of a political movement, but in many ways the movement's successfully guiding imagination, intellectual and figurative energy reseeing and rethinking the terrain common to whites and non-whites."[8]

The "fury for liberty," which Harding has rightly identified as so vital to the cultural work of the black struggle, or its Cultural Front, invigorated the whole of the Movement, notably its civil, political, social, and economic dimensions.[9] Individuals as diverse as legal champion Charles H. Houston, grassroots partisan Ella Baker, world-renowned freedom fighter Paul Robeson, and South Carolina literacy and political activist Septima Clark all shared this passion. Likewise, crucial collective actions such as the various boycotts against Jim Crow streetcars in the early twentieth century, the early 1940s March on Washington campaign, the Montgomery bus boycott (1955–56), the sit-ins and freedom rides of the early 1960s, King's ill-fated Poor People's March in 1968, and the early 1970s efforts to establish an independent black political party all exuded this furious passion for freedom.

The notion of African-American culture, like the concept of Black Power culture, or more recently hip-hop culture, grows out of contested and constructed notions of race and culture. These intricacies further intensify problems surrounding the definition of, control over, ownership of, and profits from black culture. On one hand, what exactly is it that is being defined, controlled, owned, and profited from? What makes it black? On the other hand, even once we affirm what constitutes black culture, problems persist. A crucial complication is the ignoble history of white theft and appropriation of black culture. In the context of the Black Freedom Struggle, notably the Civil Rights–Black Power Insurgency, that history has loomed large and has pushed black cultural politics toward militant forms of cultural nationalism.

A guiding assumption here is that black cultural politics, notably as showcased in black expressive culture, offers an illuminating window into modern black consciousness, or, more precisely, into the black social imagination. This black collective imagination, social imagination, or consciousness is rooted in activism rather than fantasy. Another vital aspect of the black social imagination is its emphasis on self-definition, self-fashioning, or what Arjun Appadurai terms "self-imagining."[10]

In the first essay I look at the tangled relationship between the African-American nation and the American nation in the context of the modern African-American Freedom Struggle. The aim is to get at the enduring vitality of the American idea as metaphor as well as inspiration. A paradox braces the argument. The paradox is that the idea of America has come to transcend race and culture, even as that very idea has simultaneously exemplified both race and culture.

The second essay explores black music as a pivotal terrain for black cultural politics. The integrated emphasis on historical context and cultural context makes for an essay in cultural history rather than a musicological analysis.[11]

The third and final essay takes up the problem of self-fashioning through the lenses of authenticity and representation. The argument is that while it is quite possible to describe, even define, what one means by blackness, the very processes of describing and defining, not to mention the results, are complex. As a result, in spite of continuing efforts to essentialize, even fossilize, notions of black authenticity and representation, these notions resist such fixity.

The central theme of the last essay—the resistance of black cultural politics to absolutist and essentialized notions of blackness—unites the essays. Ultimately, the search for blackness is neither merely racial, cultural, nor national. Instead, this search profoundly demonstrates a deep-seated human need for social connection and identification. Robin D. G. Kelley has argued that at their best, recent African-American identity politics are "'radical humanist' at their core and potentially emancipatory for all of us."[12] This "radical humanist" vision aptly describes the cultural politics of the Civil Rights–Black Power era. Rather than narrowly racial in goal and result, these expansive struggles have laid the necessary groundwork for a truly visionary cultural politics. In other words, they expand the reach of freedom, equality, and justice.

CHAPTER 1

"I, Too, Sing America"

Black Cultural Politics and the National Question

IN HIS POEM "My Blackness Is the Beauty of This Land," Lance Jeffers vividly captured the Black Freedom Struggle of the late 1950s. Speaking to a determined black mood spawned by World War II and the lingering residue of its hopeful rhetoric, Jeffers spoke of "my blackness, tender and strong, wounded and wise" as "this land's salvation."[1] This enduring belief that the ultimate success of the American nation necessitated the triumph of the African-American Liberation Struggle has been a fundamental assumption of that struggle. Since the founding of the United States in the late eighteenth century, the Black Freedom Struggle has seen its success as crucial to the full realization of the American national project. As with the larger American nation, the African-American nation has represented itself in religious terms as the "saving remnant," the "redeemer nation" within a nation. Speaking in a far more distinctive voice, however, the African-American nation has also represented itself as a race-based "nation within a nation."

Central to the national history of African Americans, therefore, is a self-defined dual vision of themselves as at once a vital

part of the American nation and a unique African-American nation within the American nation. While analytically separable,
these dueling yet related visions have in fact over time fed off of
each other, complicating the national history of African Americans. A striking paradox, then, has decisively shaped the nationalist history of African Americans in the United States. African
Americans as a people have historically seen themselves as both
essential to and separate from the American nation. Nevertheless,
the African American has continuously demanded that the
United States, in a very real sense "the parent nation," live up to
its emancipatory, democratic, and egalitarian promise. This ongoing African-American struggle "to redeem the soul of America"
has gone hand in hand with realizing black freedom.[2]

With this enduring paradox as the framework, the historical
travail of the Jeffers poem becomes clearer. In speaking of "to
wrench tears from which the lies would suck the salt to make me
more American than America," Jeffers goes directly to the heart
of the African-American national dilemma. Precisely because African Americans have endured and transcended the horrors of
slavery, white supremacy, and Jim Crow, they have had a con-
flicted, at times antagonistic, relationship to the American nation. They have vigorously embraced the American promise, its
sense of hope and possibility, all the while rejecting its antiblack
racism. Indeed black faith in the ideal of America has buttressed
the black struggle against the all-too-often horrific reality of
America. The fact that black America has historically waged war
against a hegemonic white supremacist America has made their
freedom struggle all the more revealing.

Jeffers concludes his poem on a bittersweet note: "yet my love
and yet my hate shall civilize this land."[3] This arresting ambivalence reveals a discerning African-American sensibility perhaps
best characterized as a dissident Americanism: a species of Americanism at once critical, progressive, inclusive, and democratic.
This particular species of Americanism has featured several inter-

active and often conflicting layers. On one level, this dissident Americanism demonstrates a deep-seated African-American hope regarding the American nation. On another level, this Americanism reflects an equally deep-seated African-American ambivalence regarding the American nation. On yet another level, this complex Americanism reveals a comparable disgust with and consequent alienation from that very same project. Hope, ambivalence, and alienation—singly and in various combinations—have thus powerfully shaped the African-American experience.

Though severely diminished, a modicum of hope persisted even during the depths of despair of the Great Depression. Even though the fog lifted a bit during World War II, those pivotal years also revealed the inveterate tensions among black hope, black ambivalence, and black alienation. Black institutions like the extended family and the church as well as the New Deal in concert with the inspirational rhetoric of President Franklin D. Roosevelt and First Lady Eleanor Roosevelt took the edge off of some of the worst hardship. Still, those at the bottom of the socioeconomic order, like blacks, suffered most. Racist discrimination within New Deal programs such as the Agricultural Adjustment Administration, which largely ignored the concerns of sharecroppers, only exacerbated that suffering.

World War II buoyed black hope as the enormous expansion in wartime jobs contributed to a second Great Migration of southern blacks. Whereas the first Great Migration saw southern blacks going mostly to the North, the second during World War II saw them going west as well. The highly ideological character of World War II likewise fed black hope. The idea that America was waging an international war against racism and fascism highlighted America's own racial quagmire. With the force of growing black support behind him, A. Philip Randolph's threatened 1941 march on Washington to protest antiblack job discrimination in defense industries eventually led President Roosevelt to act to prevent the march. His Executive Order 8802 forbade discrimination in defense industries on the basis of "race, creed, color, or national origin." Unfortunately, the Fair Employment Practices Committee that was set up to monitor complaints of discrimination lacked effective enforcement power.

Early on the global war against white supremacy and fascism emboldened a double-edged black-led campaign against the same forces at home. This Double Victory Campaign was trumpeted by the black press and built upon an increasingly aggressive collective black spirit. Further evidence of that spirit could be seen in the phenomenal growth in black membership in the National Association for the Advancement of Colored People (NAACP) during the war.

Continuing racist discrimination, however, undercut black hope and fed black ambivalence and black alienation during World War II. The demands of wartime patriotism meant that black militancy, especially among the black press, could extend only so far. Blacks certainly could not even appear to be disloyal. Nevertheless, simmering black discontent boiled over in a series of domestic racial conflagrations, capped by the Detroit race riot of 1943. That riot lasted well over thirty hours, left twenty-five blacks and nine whites dead, resulted in thousands of dollars of property damage, and required 6,000 troops called in by President Roosevelt before civic order could be restored.[4]

Black press coverage of the galling mistreatment black soldiers all too often endured under racist white officers and on Jim Crow bases led to innumerable outbreaks and only fed black anger. Many times black soldiers found themselves unofficially fighting the enemy within—a racist white military as well as racist white civilians—as well as the official enemies. The fact that German prisoners of war could eat and unwind, whereas black soldiers could not, embittered untold numbers of blacks. Because they moved too slowly out of a white waiting room in a Kentucky railroad station, three black WACs were beaten by a civilian policeman. A white South Carolina policeman gouged out the eyes of a black uniformed soldier after a heated argument. The chilling spectacle of a number of black soldiers being lynched while still in uniform crystallized why the war and its aftermath only intensified black outrage.[5]

Yet wartime and postwar black migration led to rapidly expanding black communities in the North and the West. This explosive growth not only contributed to housing shortages and related problems; it also revitalized these communities culturally and socially, bringing together black Americans from diverse southern backgrounds. The remaking of a black communal sensibility that Henry Louis Gates Jr. has noted among black soldiers from diverse backgrounds could also be observed in postwar black communities throughout the United States, especially in the West and North. During the war, Gates observed, like countless other blacks, his father "encountered the customs and sayings, the myths and folklore, of all sorts of black people he had never even heard about. The war did more to recement black American culture, which migration had fragmented, than did any other single event or experience."[6] The ongoing expansion of distinctive black communities during the 1950s, 1960s, and 1970s furthered both the complexity and remaking of black culture. It is indeed this multifaceted and shifting black culture that embraced and contributed to the emergence of the modern Black Freedom Struggle.

Evidence of black hope could be found in the successful anti–Jim Crow legal campaign waged by the NAACP beginning in the 1930s. Pioneered by a team of lawyers featuring then Howard Law School dean Charles Houston and skillfully deployed largely by Howard-trained lawyers like Thurgood Marshall and Robert L. Carter, the campaign's capstone was the 1954 *Brown* decision. Having created a cadre of highly skilled black civil rights lawyers committed to overturning the cruel fiction of "separate but equal" worlds codified by *Plessy* (1896), the *Brown* victory reflected several triumphs. The legal death knell of *Plessy* was crucial. Separate black and white schools—and by implication the entire edifice of Jim Crow—were rendered unconstitutional. In addition, the training of a cadre of black civil rights lawyers committed to advancing the Black Freedom Struggle demonstrated a firm commitment to using law as a form of judicial activism or social engineering. Equally important, working within the legal wing of the NAACP, these lawyers made legal battle a vital part of the evolving Civil Rights Movement.[7]

Similar evidence of hope could be found among the returning veterans all across the country whose all-too-often negative wartime experiences fired their commitment to the Black Freedom Struggle. From legal activist Robert Carter to political activists like Mississippi's Aaron Henry and Medgar Evers to North Carolina's Robert Williams, this development proved crucial.[8] Postwar desegregation of the armed forces initiated by President Harry Truman was also a step in the right direction.

The Montgomery bus boycott (1955–56) kicked into high gear the grassroots insurgency of the modern Black Freedom Struggle. For over a year ordinary black folk stayed off the city's busses to protest Jim Crow policies. The success there and in subsequent nonviolent direct-action campaigns throughout the South highlighted extensive grassroots activism and pushed to the fore the leadership of Martin Luther King Jr. and foot soldiers like Fannie Lou Hamer. At the same time, the "Great Repression" that followed the Great Depression and World War II undercut the radicalism of the evolving Black Freedom Struggle.[9] The anticommunist, antiradical, and antiprogressive Cold War offensive that took firm hold in the 1950s pushed the rapidly emerging Civil Rights Movement away from radicalism, notably political and economic radicalism, toward a more reformist civil rights agenda. As the 1950s anticommunist hysteria meant the "blacklisting" of radicals with procommunist sympathies, such as W. E. B. Du Bois and Paul Robeson, it also meant the narrowing of ideological and strategic alternatives within the Black Freedom Struggle.

Ups and downs thus pushed the oscillating black spirit between hope, ambivalence, and alienation. The hope of the *Brown* decision was defeated by the evasive Supreme Court enforcement decree (1955) that schools be integrated with "all deliberate speed." In reality, intense white opposition and tempered black support stymied even modest school integration until the late 1960s and early 1970s. Other forms of integration, especially in housing, proceeded even more cautiously, effectively stymied by equal—if not greater—white opposition.

The hopes of *Brown* and the Montgomery bus boycott were likewise undercut by horrific moments like the 1955 lynching of fourteen-year-old Emmett Till in Money, Mississippi, for allegedly having whistled at or spoken in a "familiar way" to a white woman (use of the term "hey baby"). The subsequent miscarriage of justice in which the white murderers went free only heightened the international disgust. The shocking photo of Till's grossly disfigured and bloated corpse that went around the world highlighted the episode's notoriety and the fear and dread the episode engendered among blacks.[10]

The modern Black Freedom Struggle thus oscillated between highs and lows. On one hand, there were moments like the huge high of the 1960 black student-led sit-in movement leading to the creation of the Student Non-Violent Coordinating Committee—the student wing of the mounting Black Liberation Insurgency. On the other hand, there were moments like the terrible low created by the murders of leaders like Malcolm X in 1965 and King in 1968 and foot soldiers like Andrew Goodman, James Chaney, and Michael Schwerner during the 1964 Mississippi Freedom Summer Campaign.

Mississippi sharecropper-turned-activist Fannie Lou Hamer plumbed the depths of the crosscutting tension between black hope, black ambivalence, and black alienation toward America in her electrifying televised address before the Credentials Committee of the Democratic National Convention in August 1964 in Atlantic City. After detailing the terrible brutality at the heart of white Mississippi's oppression of black Mississippi, notably the extreme repression she and her family endured because of her political activism, she plaintively asked: "Is this America?"[11]

That triangular friction among hope, ambivalence, and alienation also coursed throughout Martin Luther King Jr.'s classic statement of the American idea: his "I Have a Dream" speech at the 1963 March on Washington for Jobs and Freedom.[12] In that powerful effort, King captured the ceaseless conflict between black faith in the ideal America and black struggle within and against the all-too-real America of antiblack racism. This continuing clash among hope, ambivalence, and alienation notwithstanding, most blacks during the high tide of the Civil Rights years between 1955 and 1965 saw themselves as Americans, albeit dissident Americans.

As a result, in 1969, when the Impressions, featuring Curtis Mayfield, sang "This Is My Country," they hit a resonant note. Afro-Americans, they assured their audience, had labored long and hard and thus earned at too steep a price their citizenship. "I paid 300 years or more, of slave-driving sweat and welts on my back." All Americans had to be reminded of the enduring Black Freedom Struggle stretching back to resistance to slavery and forward to resistance to institutionalized racism. "Too many have died in protecting my pride, for me to go second class." Echoing back to Abraham Lincoln's prophetic warning that a house divided against itself could not stand, the conclusion the Impressions offered for America in the midst of the Movement was equally inescapable. "Shall we perish unjust or live equal as a nation?"[13]

In the latter half of the 1960s, however, both the Black Freedom Struggle and the attendant consciousness of African Americans shifted dramatically. Building upon the focus on basic human rights, nonviolent protest, and legalism in the Civil Rights years (1945–1965), the Black Power Movement expanded its emphases. The Black Power years (1965–1975) featured community empowerment, self-defense, and varieties of nationalism, including revolutionary formations like the Black Panther Party. During the Black Power years, black cultural politics reflected and fed the increasing audacity and militancy of that moment of intensifying struggle.

The conflicting feelings that blacks felt regarding the American nation moved more and more toward alienation in the Black Power years. In 1968, when Marvin E. Jackmon (Nazzam Al Fitnah) talked of "being sick and tired" of wandering about "lost in the wilderness of white America," he echoed a common and escalating sense of black estrangement. His poem "Burn, Baby, Burn" conjured up the rage and violence fueling the black urban insurrections of the late 1960s. At the time, many observers—white and black—predicted an apocalyptic interracial conflict. As late as 1974, troubadour Gil Scott-Heron admonished Afro-Americans that "the revolution will not be televised." Consequently, blacks had to reject television's hypnotic sway and, by implication, all manifestations of mass-mediated brainwashing. Scott-Heron maintained that once blacks saw America clearly through their own eyes, they indeed would "be in the streets looking for a brighter day."[14]

Yet the modern Civil Rights–Black Power Movement was far more than an extraordinary moment in the mid to late twentieth-century history of the United States. It was also an integral part of the domestic and international wave of liberation struggles of nations of color of the "Third World," like India and Ghana, against the white, Western nations of the "First World," like the United States. Geopolitically speaking, blacks in the United States in this period increasingly saw their struggle as more than just an isolated domestic struggle for civil rights. Popular black support in the 1930s for Ethiopia in its struggle to beat back the Italian invasion spoke to an increasingly widespread pan-African sentiment among a wide range of blacks, particularly discernible in the black church and the black press. The Council of African Affairs (1937–1952), with leadership that included Paul Robeson and W. E. B. Du Bois, helped spearhead the growing linkage of anticolonialism and anti-imperialism with the concurrent Black Freedom Struggle. With the onset of the anticommunist and Cold War crusade in the 1940s and 1950s, however, the modern Black Freedom Struggle made an uncomfortable peace with that crusade. As a result, that struggle shifted its focus toward civil rights and away from an aggressive anticolonial, anti-imperial, and economic critique.[15]

When that pan-African, global emphasis reemerged in the Black Freedom Struggle, it not only picked up steam, it also sought to break out of the Cold War straightjacket. This revitalized pan-African emphasis blossomed during the Black Power years, notably within the Black Panther Party in the late 1960s and early 1970s. During the late 1960s, Malcolm X's emphasis on human rights and internationalizing the "Negro's" struggle, King's opposition to the war in Vietnam, and Ella Baker's support for Puerto Rican independence were significant. These and like developments reflected a renewed black grassroots awareness of the interconnectedness of these worldwide freedom struggles among nations of color. This black internationalism had likewise found expression in widespread black interest in and support for African independence movements, especially that of Ghana, which in 1957 became the first African nation to achieve its independence, in this instance from Great Britain. That internationalism also extended to early black interest in and support for the Cuban Revolution.[16]

The various post–World War II liberation struggles of peoples of color at home and abroad fed off of each other in intriguing and often influential ways. The defeat of European colonialism and the establishment of independent nations of color through-out the world interacted symbiotically with the liberation strug-gles of Native Americans, Latino Americans, and Asian Ameri-cans as well as African Americans in the United States. These world-historical developments outside the United States, such as the success of India's anticolonial struggle against Britain, both inspired and instructed peoples of color in the United States, es-pecially African Americans.

By the high tide of the radical 1960s, communities of color in the United States represented, and in fact came to see themselves as, a kind of domestic "Third World." Within the Native Ameri-can Movement, the Chicano Movement, the Puerto Rican Movement, the Asian-American Movement, as well as the Afri-can-American Movement, there were significant sectors that saw themselves as internal colonies. According to this perspective, the liberation struggles of these domestic colonies were seeking to throw off the shackles of "First World" domination, especially white American domination. The decolonization and reconstitu-tion of the nations of color as well as the minds of peoples of color were key elements of these global, "Third World" social move-ments. Remaking these nations and minds was thus seen as re-lated to the corresponding history of black cultural struggle, and of black cultural politics in particular.[17]

Especially important for the refashioning of African-American history, culture, and identity in postwar America was a thorough-going reassessment of the African American's relationship to Africa. As Countee Cullen's famous Harlem Renaissance poem "Heritage" put the question:

> What is Africa to me:
> Copper sun or scarlet sea . . .[18]

In other words, was Africa a positive or negative referent in Afri-can-American consciousness? For African Americans caught up in the cultural revitalization of the Black Power Movement the answer was clear; it was the positive brilliance signified by the "copper sun." While sensitive to the highs and lows of the African continent's complex history, African Americans had to have the critical yet positive identification that would enable them to resolve that "proudly we can be Africans." The struggle to achieve this kind of identification, however, has been neither easy nor an unqualified success.[19]

In essence the ties between African Americans and their African roots had to be both historicized and valorized. Ordinary black Americans had to recognize their ties to the African Diaspora. In light of worldwide and long-standing notions and structures of white supremacy, Africans on the continent and throughout the diaspora have consistently had to deal with a massive anti-African assault. The histories of racist exploitation of African peoples around the world, exemplified by the history of Western colonialism and imperialism in Africa and the neocolonial dependency of postcolonial Africa, have only magnified the problem, as have racist representations of Africans and African histories and cultures in the West, especially the United States. As evidenced by the pan-African politics of the Black Power Movement and twentieth-century pan-Africanism more generally, a usable black past and a viable black future demanded that the humanity and dignity of all African peoples, on the continent and throughout the diaspora, be fully respected. This aspect of the struggle can be glimpsed in the creation of Black Studies departments. It could also be seen in the positive embrace of Africa in the cultural politics of black power.

This engagement with Africanness leads directly to considerations of identity in all its complexity. A crucial part of the historical development of the identities of peoples of color has been the broader issue of shifts in identities and cultures in the larger cultural matrix of both postwar America and the postwar world. As a result, the modern Black Liberation Insurgency both influenced and showed the influence of fundamental shifts throughout American culture.

Throughout this period, the incisive historical critique of the American Dream lived and affirmed by blacks came to be increasingly shared by innumerable Americans. As blacks showed the way, this critique included youthful rebellion, a growing appreciation of diversity and difference, an increasing commitment to notions of community as against individualism, a shift toward idealism, and a search for spiritual and moral clarity. This dissident black-inspired Americanism railed against what Jennifer Hochschild has described as "the hollowness of materialism, the denigration of community, the hypocrisy of claims to equal opportunity, the selfishness of the lucky."[20]

Before the late 1960s, the most common term of reference for peoples of African descent in the United States was "Negro." Between 1945 and 1965, a key aspect of the gathering "Negro" liberation struggle was the rearticulation of what it meant to be a "Negro American." As previously noted, this was a profoundly cultural—as well as civil, political, social, and economic—issue. Related and equally vital to this process of redefinition was the foundational issue of identity: the relationship of Negroes to one another as individuals and as a collectivity, to other Americans, to the American nation-state, and, finally, to the broader world. This was not a novel issue, though. In fact these concerns, especially the relationship of blacks to Africa as well as America, have engaged African Americans throughout their American experience.

As African Americans rearticulated a sense of cultural and psychological identity between 1945 and 1975, what transpired was a common historical and intergenerational pattern. Each subsequent generation has stood upon the shoulders of its ancestors and endeavored to build a better future for itself and its progeny. For African Americans striving for autonomy and self-definition within a white-dominated society, this has often been a difficult challenge. Yet, "for every generation of blacks since Emancipation," Lawrence Levine has reminded us, "the idea of the New Negro, in all its varying forms, has been a crucial rallying cry and a source of great optimism and ego gratification."[21] During the Civil Rights years (1945–65) and Black Power years (1965–1975), the "New Negroes" searchingly reassessed and, after considerable deliberation, reasserted the inherent African-American relationship to the United States even as they often drew closer to their African roots. Black Americans thus reiterated their American identity notwithstanding their often deeply troubled historical relationship with America.

The traditional view of the Civil Rights Movement has stressed the prominent, albeit contested, strategy of integration as the Movement's fundamental meaning. The history of integration during this era vividly demonstrates the dissident Americanism exuded by African Americans—at once critical, progressive, inclusive, and democratic. This emphasis on integration as a central goal of the Black Freedom Struggle illustrates equally well the deeply vexed black relationship to the American nation-state.

The view of integration as the Movement's central goal reflects the fact that the destruction of Jim Crow was the Movement's essence. Integration represented the final racial frontier: the full acceptance of blacks as American citizens. From this point of view, the guiding dilemma was at least threefold. Confirming whether integration would lead to the creation of truly color-blind institutions and structures constituted one aspect of the dilemma. Another aspect consisted in confirming whether integration merely reinforced white power and white supremacy at the expense of not just black power, but also democracy and equality. A third element of the dilemma, in many ways the most salient, was the extent to which integration embraced blacks on their own terms. In other words, to what extent would integration embrace black culture and blackness more generally? As Stokely Carmichael and Charles V. Hamilton argued in *Black Power*, "maintenance of black pride and black cultural integrity" were essential.[22] Similarly, to what extent would all black institutions, black community-based officials, and black leaders be part of an integrated society? To what extent would the positive features of voluntary black segregation be maintained? To what extent would the larger political and economic system be effectively integrated?

Concurrent notions of integration varied widely, ranging from token white acceptance of exceptional blacks to the vision of economic equality as necessary. Today integration remains an ambiguous notion and, as a consequence, a notion unrealized. Between 1945 and 1975, the development of integration as idea and practice was slow and halting at best. The key symbolic register of integration—school integration as mandated by the *Brown* decision (1954)—witnessed limited and checkered progress, except, ironically, in the South, where federal mandates and intervention to enforce school integration in the late 1960s and 1970s began to make a difference. By the late twentieth century, however, even much of that limited progress was unraveling as resegregation took hold.

While integration was thus undeniably important, intense white opposition to integration, in the North and West as well as the South, and intense black anxiety about integration undermined it as a vision, not to mention as a policy. The failure of integration could be seen in many places, from entrenched patterns of job discrimination to the intransigence of residential segregation. Thus, while affirmative action programs in the late 1960s and the 1970s provided opportunity for a limited yet significant number of blacks to begin to achieve noteworthy levels of upward mobility, the structures of white privilege and inequality persisted.

While integration was undeniably important, the more flexible strategy of pluralism was much more sensitive to the imperatives of black cultural and historical distinctiveness. In fact a key aspect of Black Power ideology was the argument that power in the American system was group-based rather than individual-based.

As a result, group power typically constrained individual power. As individuals, therefore, blacks could rise only to the extent that black power grew stronger. Again, as Carmichael and Hamilton observed: "Black Power recognizes—it must recognize—the ethnic basis of American Politics as well as the power-oriented nature of American politics. Black Power therefore calls for black people to consolidate behind their own, so that they can bargain from a position of strength."[23] Pluralism meant the full acceptance of group-based power as expressive and protective of the individual rights and responsibilities of those belonging to the particular group, in this case blacks. Pluralism embraced desegregation, a more voluntaristic and incentive-driven variety of integration. Consequently, pluralism proved in reality a far more viable strategic aim among African Americans themselves.

Similarly, the traditional view of the Black Power movement sees racial nationalism or racial separatism at its center. Several varieties of this point of view abounded at the time, including notions of internally driven black community empowerment, a separate black nation-state within the southern United States, and African-American repatriation to Africa. While the strategies of integration and separatism characterized both the Civil Rights and Black Power movements in important ways, both strategies must be understood for what they were at the time: strategic means toward ends rather than ends in and of themselves. They were markers, but not the definitive markers.

The crux of the matter was how best to advance the relationship of blacks to the American project: how best to achieve the classic American notions of freedom, equality, and justice. In the context of the postwar African-American Freedom Struggle, this meant coming to grips with Negroness (1945–1965) and blackness (1965–1975) as fundamentally American. This also meant the reverse: coming to grips with America as fundamentally African and black.

The Civil Rights and Black Power years witnessed a profound

African-American cultural revitalization moment—a powerful reorientation in beliefs, values, and, therefore, behaviors. This revitalization process encompassed historical, activist, visionary, and identity-related developments. One key development was the work of validating a rich and sustaining black culture and past on its own terms. This move necessitated clarifying and examining the African and New World roots and transformations of African Americans. Another central development in this revitalization was using foundational history and culture as a means to construct a more positive American present and to envision a more hopeful American future. This revitalization moment echoed the New Negro Renaissance of the 1920s in its emphasis on the development of a distinctive black aesthetic and a distinctive black cultural politics. What set the modern movement apart were its intimate relationship to the Civil Rights–Black Power Movement, its grassroots emphasis, and its widespread impact. The global dimension of this revitalization project could be seen in the growing black opposition to the Vietnam War on grounds of internationalist solidarity and the right of the Vietnamese people to self-determination as well as the solidarity of oppressed people of color, or Third World solidarity.

This modern revitalization moment likewise found blacks rearticulating a multitiered identity typically rooted in popular notions of race. Though centered in race, this multifaceted black identity radiated outward to encompass, at its best, often crosscutting identities growing out of related struggles for freedom and democracy, such as women's rights and labor struggles. As a result, this thirty-year period revealed a heightened black consciousness going in non-race-specific directions as well as race-specific ones. This could perhaps best be seen in the emergence of black feminist concerns that refused to subordinate gender to race. Instead a black feminist consciousness viewed the multiple axes of identity, including class and sexuality, as mutually dependent and inseparable in terms of the lived experience of black women.

The 1960s/1970s revitalization moment built upon the 1920s New Negro Renaissance, or Harlem Renaissance, in its emphasis on the development of a distinctive black aesthetic and a distinctive black cultural politics. The revitalization movement also built upon the continuing politicization of culture spawned by the Depression. This evolving entanglement with black cultural politics revealed a persistent and heightened concern with issues of the role of black artists and cultural warriors more generally in this time of severe economic crisis.

Harlem institutions like painter Charles Alston's Harlem Art Workshop, later his 306 Workshop, and sculptor Augusta Savage's Studio of Arts and Crafts allowed young visual artists like painter Jacob Lawrence to grapple with a range of issues, including issues of aesthetics and technique. The 306 Workshop was noted for its heady mix of artists, including Aaron Douglas (the most famous artist of the Harlem Renaissance) and future artistic great Romare Bearden as well as Lawrence. Writers included Langston Hughes, Claude McKay, and Ralph Ellison. Elizabeth M. Turner has noted that "the struggle for self-portrayal by the African-American community—indeed the desire to be born anew in the eyes of the world and to contribute powerfully to what it meant to be American—set the tone and direction of the Harlem Workshops."[24]

This politicization of culture also owed much to the impact of the Communist-inspired Popular Front of the 1930s and 1940s. Even here, in spite of the primacy attached to economic and material forces in history, the centrality of cultural struggle to progressive social movements and grassroots political mobilization was increasingly acknowledged. This "radical social-democratic movement forged around anti-fascism, anti-lynching, and the industrial unionism of the CIO," as Michael Denning has shown, encompassed many non–Communist Party Members, Party members, and "'fellow travelers' with greater or lesser degrees of affiliation to the Party."[25] Most notable in this context were world-renowned entertainer and activist Paul Robeson and literary leading light and activist Langston Hughes. The centrality of black cultural politics is likewise shown in the ways in which Alabama's 1930s black Communists made Communist ideology relevant to their own lives, in effect recasting that ideology. As Robin D. G. Kelley has demonstrated, a "radical, prophetic tradition of Christianity was a major factor in drawing blacks into the Communist Party and its mass organizations."[26]

A vigorous 1960s black cultural reawakening built upon the intense black politicization, or political awakening, of the Movement itself in two ways. First, there was the audacious assertion of Negroness and blackness as historical advances—cognitive and cultural leaps. Constituting these moves as empowering and progressive brought forth a plethora of theories and practices, many of which animated the Black Arts movement specifically and various expressions of black cultural nationalism more broadly. Second, there was an increasingly popular, or grassroots, nationalist position, especially during the Black Power years. The overriding aim of this position was to define and then to constitute the disparate African-American communities in the United States as a meaningful singular nation, substantively as well as rhetorically. Generally speaking, creating Negroness and blackness and imagining the African-American nation were interlocking positions.

Crafting racialized identities and building a black nation necessitated African-American self-definition and African-American control. All kinds of efforts to enhance black autonomy and to eradicate white domination proliferated. Similarly, various and sundry attempts to promote what its proponents saw as a positive, black-defined sense of black identity and to root out a negative white-defined sense of black identity grew. Throughout it all, the dominant concerns were group identity and group power.

The historical problem of African-American cultural identity thus provides much-needed insight into modern American culture and consciousness as well as African-American culture and consciousness. At midcentury, a vital yet often ill-understood and dimly perceived battle was brewing over whether, historically speaking, there was any such phenomenon as a distinctive and viable African-American culture. *An American Dilemma*—the highly influential World War II study of black-white relations in the United States authored by Swedish economist Gunnar Myrdal—epitomized the dominant view. Myrdal observed: "In practically all of its divergences, American Negro culture is not something independent of general American culture. It is a distorted development, or a pathological condition, of the general American culture."[27]

The notion of the fundamental Americanness of "American Negro culture" was on the mark. However, the common mid-century view that "American Negro culture" constituted a distorted or pathological development was wrong, invidious, and dangerous. This erroneous view fundamentally denied black agency, not to mention black humanity. In turn, it reinforced white supremacy. The oppositional view reflected the growing popular as well as social scientific influence of cultural relativism. According to this notion, a group's culture had to be evaluated contextually, according to its meanings and functions for the group itself, not according to outside criteria. As a result, for crosscultural discussions to proceed, they had to be framed in terms of equivalence or commensurability rather than in terms of hierarchy or ethnocentrism (or racism).

From this vantage point, African-Americans possessed not just a culture, but a healthy and viable culture. This minority view was persuasively argued in the pioneering yet often undervalued work of anthropologists such as Zora Neale Hurston and Melville J. Herskovits. In fact the role of anthropology, especially African-American anthropology, in pushing forward this view has been critical. In addition, at midcentury, cultural warriors like Hurston and Langston Hughes reflected the increasingly widespread concurrent acceptance of a positive view of black culture, notably black folk culture, among blacks themselves.

This evolving grassroots black acceptance of the strength and viability of their own culture was linked inextricably to the growing Black Freedom Struggle. This linkage could be seen in the "New Negro" radicalism of the 1920s, epitomized by the elite Harlem Renaissance and the mass-based Marcus Garvey Universal Negro Improvement Association. It could subsequently be seen in black militancy during the Depression and World War II, a militancy clearly linked to previous expressions of militancy, notably that of the 1920s.

The aggressive and affirmative cultural politics of the modern Black Freedom Struggle forced a national about-face regarding the existence and viability of black culture. Put another way, a widespread, complicated, and multileveled black cultural insurgency contributed powerfully to the success of the Black Freedom Struggle. From a social scientific perspective, the successful refutation of the cultural deficit model and the culture of poverty thesis proved important. African-American culture, therefore, was neither stunted nor diminished in shape and substance. Furthermore, the unconscionably high levels of poverty and economic discrimination endured by blacks influenced, but did not undermine, black culture. In the historical literature, the demonstration of viable slave cultures and viable slave communities paved the way for the reinterpretation of postslavery African-American cultures and communities in a far more insightful light.[28]

The salient point was clear and compelling. Historically, African-American culture had helped sustain the ongoing Black Freedom Struggle, often against seemingly insuperable odds. During the Black Power years in particular, everything from greetings and handshakes to hairstyles and walks reiterated the centrality and force of cultural struggle. Popular music and poetry in particular reiterated black cultural viability and pride. "Black is beautiful" was not just an empty slogan or an aesthetic conceit, but an imperative of black cultural politics in the age of Black Power.[29] It was a slogan resonant with a range of meanings and consequences, some positive and some not so positive.

Not surprisingly, however, with the contested victory affirming the significance and viability of black culture, in many ways the battle had just begun. In particular, there remained substantive disagreement among blacks themselves over how best to characterize and assess black culture(s). What were its defining features, and what were the shape and meaning of its history? Just how separate, American, or African, was it? How did class enter into the mix? In other words, to what degree have lower-, middle-, and upper-class African Americans shared a homologous culture? Similarly, how did other forms of difference within black communities—such as gender, sexual orientation, skin color, religion, and place (geography, region, location: urban, rural; North, South, East, West)—impinge upon definitions of black culture? The key question remained whether or not, differences notwithstanding, there was enough organic unity in the concept of a black culture, or more accurately perhaps, of black cultures, to render it, or them, conceptually and analytically viable.

While all of these issues are important to an understanding of black history, culture, and identity in postwar America, the most critical is making sense of the symbiotic relationship between these three interrelated areas and American history, culture, and identity. An absolutely essential ingredient of the modern African-American Liberation Insurgency was the bold and inspiring quest to realize an America truer to its best self. Likewise essential was the equally bold and inspiring quest to understand black history, culture, and identity as central not just to a race-based nationalism or an Afrocentric project, but also—and even more revealing—as a defining feature of the evolving American project.

The revitalization of African-American struggle and consciousness thus went in several different yet related directions at once, constituting a multileveled and dynamic process. Simultaneously, this escalating insurgent spirit found expression in innumerable theories and practices, clustering around four dominant and overlapping positions: first, Negroness, blackness; second, Africanness, notably pan-Africanism; third, separateness, or black nationalism; and fourth, Americanness, or American nationalism. Negroness/blackness referred to an American- or New World–rooted identity or sensibility, while Africanness referred to an African or Old World one. Whereas black nationalism signifies the struggle to create a black nation within or outside the American nation, American nationalism signifies a white-dominated nation seeking to come to grips with its multicultural reality and multicultural constituencies.

Each of these related yet distinctive positions yielded salient points of view and developments impinging upon African-American history, culture, and identity. The revitalization dynamic revealed a set of core goals common to each position: the enhancement of black self-image and the alleviation of self-hatred, fatalism, and nihilism; the reclamation of lost, neglected, and unknown roots; and the creation—whenever necessary—of new modes of racial identification. While these aims had been advanced before with considerable impact, especially during the 1920s with Garveyism and the Harlem Renaissance, the far more powerful Civil Rights–Black Power Insurgency gave them a far greater urgency and impact in the 1960s and 1970s.

Blackness, Africanness, black nationalism, and American nationalism were all grand and serious adventures. Blackness found particularly compelling expression around the hotly contested markers of race, skin color, gender, sexuality, economic and social notions of class, and place. Africanness stressed reconnecting with "Mother Africa": that is, working through the enduring historical consequences of the forced exile of New World African enslavement. This growing concern with traumatic rupture and geographic estrangement fed an up-and-down pan-African sensibility—up during the Black Power years—endeavoring to restore ties between continental Africa and its displaced peoples worldwide. Successful national liberation movements in Africa and black nations around the globe directly fed this burgeoning diasporic consciousness. An influential variety of black nationalism emphasized African repatriation—a real return for a select few, and, for a far larger number, a symbolic return. This species of African-American nationalism vividly demonstrated the fertile interaction across the porous boundaries of blackness and Africanness.

An increasing sense of intrinsic difference dividing blacks from whites intensified all manner of black nationalism: political, economic, and cultural, on one side; radical/ revolutionary and rebellious/reformist, on the other.[30] Paradoxically, however, a hopeful commitment among blacks to the American project persisted, even amid the militant racial separatism and antiwhite rhetoric of the era. In other words, for most blacks, alienation from the United States rarely reached the point of a wholesale rejection of America, in spite of hyperbolic rhetoric and militant actions. When push actually came to shove, they were still Americans, even if African Americans.

It has become axiomatic to describe identity as "situational, fluid, contingent, and contextualized," observes Catherine L. Macklin. She reminds us, however, "this does not mean that identity changes into something utterly different in every different situation." Rather, "different aspects" of the multidimensional identities of racial groups like blacks "are deemed relevant," and are therefore "selected and emphasized by the actors in a given situation."[31] Consequently, as racialist and nationalist pressures within the Movement sped up, at times into overdrive, the inherent difficulties of these narrowing and limiting pressures became clearer. As a result, in ways the salience of intrablack differences became more pronounced. Therefore, when black became "beautiful" and fashionable, the results were revealing.

Intriguingly enough, a dictum of "the blacker the better" gained currency. The growing valorization of dark complexions, full lips and noses, and curly hair as markers of blackness, among models and beauty queens, for example, too often meant minimizing the complex range of physical features among blacks in favor of a stereotypical blackness. In turn, this trend led to a view of light complexions, thin noses, and straight hair among blacks as markers of racial pollution and impurity—in effect, as rendering claims to authentic blackness suspect. At times, efforts to undo the self-denying notions of black beauty rooted in white notions of beauty went overboard. Such excesses in the struggle to appreciate blackness in its full range and diversity were to be expected in a white supremacist society.[32]

As the struggle over black physical aesthetics highlights, cultural struggle represents a vital terrain within the ongoing Black Liberation Insurgency. A related and similarly pivotal concern has been to enhance African-American commitment to grassroots struggle. Identity politics becomes a vital battleground for converts willing to go the extra mile. A key assumption underlying this emphasis on African-American identity in the gathering of soldiers for the mass movement is both ideological and strategic. Seen one way, a guiding assumption is that a more positive sense of African-American self-worth braces more active affiliation with the Movement. Seen another way, black racial identification and black cultural identity, on one side, and a more positive black self-concept, on the other, were viewed as mutually dependent. In turn, both were jointly important to pushing African Americans to become part of the growing grassroots insurgency.

While the complicated question of which, if any, empirically demonstrable factors separate activists from the "shadow" movement of hangers-on, sympathizers, and passive supporters is important, the concern here is humanistic and qualitative rather than quantitative and social scientific. That focus is the mindset as well as the defining actions and thought of those who aligned themselves with the Movement. This is a shifting and broad coalition—from the zealous to the cautious, from the active to the passive, from national leaders to grassroots ones, from those operating outside the Movement proper, but within its shadow, to those who personify it.[33]

Sorting through the complex history of how African Americans have envisioned and felt about themselves is exceedingly difficult and still awaits definitive elaboration. Suffice it to say, however, that self-concept is a protean and ambiguous concept in social psychology. Historically, the evidence suggests that, collectively speaking, oppressed and marginalized groups like African Americans have been forced to endure a greater number and degree of psychosocial assaults than dominant groups like WASPs. One consequence of this brutalization is alleged to be lowered self-esteem and more self-hatred—a higher incidence of identity problems generally—among the oppressed.

While there is substantial evidence to sustain this interpretation, there is also an impressive body of conflicting evidence. It is obvious that in spite of the extraordinary obstacles African Americans have confronted—notably slavery, Jim Crow, and white supremacy—they have not as a group disintegrated. On the contrary, they have survived, often thrived, and often surmounted what has been a very hostile environment. This history of endurance and transcendence illustrates an uncommon measure of psychological health and emotional resilience.[34]

Still, it is equally clear that over the years racial oppression has exacted a horrific toll among untold numbers of African Americans, diminishing both the quality of their lives and their sense of self. The problems inherent in realizing a positive African-American self-concept, therefore, have been serious, multifaceted, and historically contingent.[35] Faced with these difficult psychosocial tensions, the black consciousness component of the postwar liberation struggle rooted in the Black Power Movement stressed the complicated intersection among individual and collective identity, self-esteem, and race pride. Those who saw expanding black consciousness as central to the African-American freedom struggle saw this battle as historical and cultural as well as psychosocial. In its innumerable, at times quixotic, efforts to advance black self-esteem and race pride, the Black Power phase of the Movement achieved a noteworthy measure of success, persistent problems notwithstanding. From this point of view, the audacious quest to imagine and in turn to create a black world was at once radical (in some ways revolutionary), positive, and affirmative: on balance, a triumph for black cultural politics.

While the black nation within the American nation has been a compelling vision for a vocal, at times influential, minority, the ideal and the real American nation-state have most decisively shaped black nationalist visions. As previously observed, the enduring problem has been how African-Americans, as a "nation within a nation," have defined themselves and developed in relation to the American experiment. While evolving out of the historical experiences of African Americans, black nationalism signifies—above all else—Africans as Americans, as a New World people. In fact the basic frame of reference and outlook of black nationalism have been quintessentially American. Leonard I. Sweet's classic characterization of nineteenth-century black nationalism cuts directly to the heart of its twentieth-century descendants.

> The direction of Black Nationalism, which manifested itself in black separatism, black solidarity, and black consciousness, was not towards exclusion from America but inclusion into American society. Black leaders were Americans, that they knew, but to secure that status they had to separate them-

selves from white Americans and assert themselves as black Americans. Black separatism, therefore, was often the means of concretizing an identity as Americans and an image of America which recognized no racial distinctions.[36]

The paradox at the core of black nationalism—a narrow racial nationalism as a means toward a broad-based and color-blind America—has only enhanced its historical complexity. This was especially the case in the postwar Black Freedom Struggle.

This interpretation neither denies nor diminishes the African component of African-American identity, for it remains real and vital. Similarly, many observers, myself included, have agreed with Sterling Stuckey that "the depths of African culture in America have been greatly underestimated by most nationalist theorists in America." And, I would add, by most Americans. In fact, as Stuckey has shown, most nationalist theorists "were exposed to main currents of African culture without understanding how those currents might contribute to the surge toward liberation they wanted to initiate." Black nationalist theorists as diverse as the nineteenth-century progenitor David Walker and the mid-twentieth-century artistic and political giant Paul Robeson have grappled mightily with this fundamental issue: the deep and continuing impact of African cultures on New World cultures in the Americas, notably African-American cultures.[37]

To reiterate: the impact of the real and imagined Africa on African-American history and culture, in particular the enduring African-American Freedom Struggle, has been profound. The argument advanced here, though, goes in a related but different direction. The argument is that by the mid-twentieth century, this pan-African connection is best understood as primarily an American phenomenon with New World, hybrid, and diasporic dimensions. The creolized histories, cultures, and identities that come to be constituted as African American are indeed necessarily both African and American. Yet given the centrality of the American context, black nationalism in the latter half of the twentieth century is first and foremost an American story.

Consequently, an inveterate yet ambivalent African-American identification with America—and in turn the United States—as a homeland persists in spite of awesome trials and tribulations. This ambivalent Americanism thus derives organically from the bittersweet historical experience of Africans in America. The Civil Rights years underscored both the ambivalence and the bittersweetness; the Black Power years brought into bold relief the hate in the ambivalence and the bitter in the bittersweet.

The Movement intensified the black attraction to and repulsion from America. This deep-seated ambivalence has often trumped the interactive trinity of hope, ambivalence, and alienation—introduced at the outset—that has earmarked the African-American experience in America. During periods of heightened social flux and social change—as during the high tide of Civil Rights–Black Power activism—the dialectical pull between revitalization and assimilation has intensified. In other words, the clash between racial distinctiveness, in this case blackness, and assimilation, or diminishing such distinctions, accelerated. The tug-of-war intensified between black cultural revitalization, notably of the nationalist variety, and assimilation, the concept of blacks melding into a mainstream white American culture and thus losing their cultural distinctiveness, losing their blackness.

Postwar black progress, fitful as it was, especially the progress spawned by the Movement, further fueled escalating black expectations and demands. "It was precisely because periods of increased opportunity and mobility posed the greatest threats to whole layers of black cultural tradition," Levine has argued, "that such periods often witnessed important manifestations of cultural revitalization."[38] Whereas assimilationists all too uncritically envisioned African Americans becoming increasingly mainstream and less ostensibly black, nationalists saw African Americans tenaciously guarding their racial distinctiveness, and thus their cultural distinctiveness, as fundamental to their history and identity as well as the Freedom Struggle itself.

The diachronic tension between assimilation and revitalization illustrates other flaws in these respective positions. The romantic whiggishness of each belies the historical complexity of the African-American experience. That experience, like history writ large, moves in various directions at once, certainly not in necessarily forward-looking, progressive, and necessarily discernible directions. Indeed, one of the critical contributions of historical writing and historians as a group is the formal imposition of shape and meaning on the messiness and polydirectionality of lived experience.

Both assimilation and revitalization cut against the grain of defining elements of the African-American experience: non-linearty, antiphony (or call and response movement), and improvisation. Both ignore the syncretic dynamic operating across boundaries between the mass, hegemonic cultural core and the extremely important component, in ways conflicting, visions that make up that core. While largely European-inflected, that core is flexible and shifting. Fundamentally hybrid, this core necessarily encompasses vital elements incorporated from African Americans and other marginalized groups. As a result, simplistic notions of assimilation and revitalization ultimately fail to account for the complicated interactions among the elements shaping America's fundamentally multicultural albeit European-American–dominated core.

Nevertheless, broadly speaking, assimilation and revitalization are very useful as ways to get at the fundamental ambivalence African Americans have historically felt and expressed toward America. This ambivalence is an American as opposed to a peculiarly African-American phenomenon. Other ethnnoracial and marginalized groups have been simultaneously repelled by and pulled toward the hegemonic cultural core, toward the ideal America. For African Americans as for others, this ambivalence is not just about the ideals and realities of America from their unique historical vantage point. This gnawing ambivalence captures the persistent paradox at the heart of these group-based struggles: that Americanization inevitably both undermines and strengthens their distinctive history and identity in subtle and not-so-subtle ways. For African Americans, this has meant a compounded ambivalence: a complicated love-hate relationship toward both halves of their dual identity as Africans and as Americans.

In terms of cultural development, the revitalization-assimilation dialectic intersects and thus influences the dialectic between innovation and tradition. The effect is syncretic and at its best synergistic. In their assimilation of different kinds of musical influences like pop and jazz to a rhythm-and-blues core, the Motown musicians revitalized that more traditional rhythm-and-blues music even as they crafted an innovative variety of the emerging soul music idiom. In the assembly-line making and marketing of the Motown Sound, "The Music of Young America," the earthier, blues-based aspects of the music had to be polished in an effort to appeal to a white-dominated crossover audience. Simultaneously, pop and jazz were affected in often telling ways: pop became blacker, and jazz's blackness deepened. Classic Motown hits like Mary Wells's "My Guy" and the Temptations' "My Girl" exemplify the impact of these crosscutting developments and their hybrid results.[39]

African-American expressive culture's embodiment of the fruits of the tension between innovation and tradition has indeed given that culture—especially its music, notably jazz—important symbolic and social power. In fact the vigor and accessibility of African-American expressive culture help explain why that culture, especially African-American music and dance, have come increasingly to serve as a defining symbol, a critical marker, for all of American culture globally as well as nationally.

The dynamic tension between tradition and innovation has

likewise fed the Black Freedom Struggle and black cultural politics. The salience of jazz as a metaphor for the vision of American culture as creole is illustrative in crucial ways of an African-American–rooted hybridity. This metaphor builds upon the process of collective improvisation essential to jazz performance: why, how, and with what consequences the individual instruments, sounds, styles, and personalities actually come together and create original music every time out. In other words, jazz signifies how the one is continuously created out of the interactions among the many: how the collectivity emerges out of its constituent elements. Jazz represents a "reconciling of opposites" for John A. Kouwenhoven. It "is the first art form," he writes, "to give full expression to Emerson's ideal of a union which is perfect only 'where all the uniters are isolated.'"[40]

In *The Jazz Cadence of American Culture*, Robert G. O'Meally has showcased the centrality of jazz to American culture. He demonstrates that throughout twentieth-century American culture, "the factor of jazz music recurs over and over again: jazz dance, jazz poetry, jazz painting, jazz film, and more. Jazz as metaphor, jazz as model, jazz as relentlessly powerful cultural influence, jazz as cross-disciplinary beat or cadence. Consider Muhammad Ali—boxing-dancing, spouting rhythmical rhymes, dramatically proclaiming a new world order in religion and politics." In a vital sense, a jazz performance par excellence! Jazz, then, is a crucial terrain for the evolution of black cultural politics. Paraphrasing Brent Edwards, O'Meally writes: "Sometimes . . . the jazz effect in culture is a way of making cultural expression political or of making political expression palpable as culture."[41] Or, as argued here, the jazz effect in culture reveals the connections between art and politics, in this case between African-American cultural work and African-American Freedom Struggle.

The postwar reconstruction of the United States as a result of the African-American Freedom Struggle yields a vastly different

America. It is a changing nation increasingly, often grudgingly, aware of its blackness and, in turn, its diversity. The shift is away from exceptionalism and whiteness toward complexity and pluralism as critical markers of American history, culture, and identity. We understand more and more that America—like its defining ideal of freedom—is a compelling yet contested vision of hope and possibility open to various and conflicting interpretations. As witnessed in the Civil Rights–Black Power years, America is constantly being made and remade. Kouwenhoven persuasively insists that "'America' is not a synonym for the United States. It is not a fixed and immutable ideal toward which citizens of this nation strive. It has not order or proportion, but neither is it chaos except as that is chaos whose components no single mind can comprehend or control. America is process."[42]

As a remarkably compelling symbol for the United States (and beyond), the idea of America speaks polyvocally, often at once. Echoing a principal line of argument advanced here, Nathan Huggins once observed: "what is most remarkable about much that is called black culture is its Americanness; and conversely, much of what is considered most uniquely American is essentially Afro-American."[43] Yet the logic of the cultural politics growing out of the modern African-American Liberation Insurgency demands getting beyond a manichean vision of American culture.

The very notion of American culture has no viable meaning outside of a multilayered and complex sense of diversity and heterogeneity. Giles Gunn has insisted that "the figure in that carpet of commingled peoples and traditions which we now describe as 'American' can only be perceived for what it is by understanding the disparate threads that in their comparative relations make it up." The United States, he further explains, is culturally

> the expression of many variant and highly variable traditions
> that still coexist within a single but ever elusive and always
> changing system of possibilities. To put this more simply, we

are now in a position to see that whatever we mean by the United States as a cultural formation, we mean nothing less than a configuration of comparable but often competing regional or sectional or otherwise minority traditions that were, and are, always seeking primacy over one another, or at least are seeking not to be displaced by one another.[44]

By centering the history, culture, and identity of African Americans, the modern Black Freedom Struggle changed America forever. Not only did it spearhead the national confrontation with its blackness, but it also spearheaded our national confrontation with our basic hybridity and diversity. As a result, there is greater awareness of the complex truth in the claim framed by Langston Hughes and shared by all his compatriots: "I, too, sing America . . . I, too, am America."[45]

CHAPTER 2

"Spirit in the Dark"

Black Music and Black Freedom

SOMETHING WASN'T QUITE RIGHT. Yes, the music sounded just fine. The band, especially the lead and rhythm guitarists, zoomed. With the drummer kicking it hard, the music's heavy bass line boomed. Their beautiful voices taking flight, the background singers soared in, through, and over it all, hitting the accents, accentuating the rhythms, weaving in and out of the melodies, crafting striking harmonies. All three by themselves sounded like a full choir. Borrowing the words of the sanctified church sisters, "they could sang y'all." In fact, they "sang" their hearts out. But in spite of a really hot performance thus far, it still wasn't kicking on all cylinders.

Intense from the outset, audience participation escalated. Heads bobbed and weaved. Hands waved, fluttered, and clapped, all in time to the driving music. Feet stomped in a variety of syncopated cadences. Singles, couples, and groups danced in the aisles and within the rows. Dance moves jumped out from everywhere: from yesterday's "Slop" and "Cha-Cha," to the more recent "Shing-a-Ling" and "Boog-a-Loo," to couples intimately entwined in a grinding "Slow Drag." Love and desire were in abundance.

Moans, groans, shouts, and screams pierced the air. "Hush your mouth!" "A-a-men!" "Tell it like it is!" "Get on down with it!" "Bring it on home, now!" "'Sang' that song real sweet, now!" Having been wired from the beginning, the audience wanted to be taken "there." Reveling in a series of up-tempo hits, the audience responded to favorite tunes, notably favorite vocal lines and licks, with frenzied outcries. "Somebody help me!" "Talk to me!" Singing along and communally reworking the tunes, audience and performer remade the songs, making them their own at that time and that place. Still, something was missing.

In "great voice," "the Queen" ruled. She sang effortlessly across octaves and keys; ascended and descended scales with reckless abandon; dramatized highs and lows with a dizzying array of moods, poses, and gestures; heedlessly snatched notes from here and there; crooned in and around melodies and vocal lines. "Blue notes," "jazz notes," "gospel notes," "pop notes" burst forth singly and in various wondrous mixes. Raw emotion, intense passion, fervent commitment, aching heartbreak, the overwhelming need to love and to be loved were everywhere. While "the Spirit" was in the house, the Queen having invoked its presence, an elusive something was nonetheless missing.

An entrancing mocha deity, the Queen was regal and radiant: an enchanting face, a short Afro coif framed by an elegant silver crown, a loose-fitting yet stunning silver gown, stylish matching silver pumps. Moving gracefully around her throne, the stage, she exuded presence and control. Thus far, she had sung mostly up-tempo numbers, working with mike in hand, "moving and grooving," flashing several popular dance moves.

Then all of a sudden, in midstream, she slowed it all down, admitting that she just didn't feel her best. All the glittering houselights were brought down to a single spotlight on the piano, another of her several thrones. For a short moment, she wept softly. Then she slowly began to play the piano, a gospel run here, a jazz run there, a blues run here, coming together in a mesmerizing rhythm and blues, or "soul," statement. Searching for solace, she cried out in song: "I Never Loved a Man (the Way I Love You)," "(You Make Me Feel like) A Natural Woman," "Share Your Love with Me," "Call Me!"

The "Spirit in the Dark" had arrived! Soul Sister Number One, the Queen of Soul, emissary of the Spirit, like the Spirit itself, was now truly "in the house."[1] From this point forward, the Queen literally "brought the house down," "wrecked the house." "Church was out!" Aretha took her flock "there," to that "Higher Ground," if only for a few fleeting moments.

Nikki Giovanni, one of the most popular poets of the day, observed at the height of the Queen's late 1960s reign that

> aretha was the riot was the leader if she had said "come
> let's do it" it would have been done.[2]

Almost thirty years later, poet Bruce Smith spoke of hearing the "Voice of Aretha in Italy." Awestruck by "the squawling of a recording," he recalled,

> and I'm on my knees for this song
> greater than a nation and a name. Amen.[3]

In "The Voice of Aretha Franklin Surprises Me," poet E. Ethelbert Miller experienced a remarkably similar epiphany in Saudi Arabia. Reaching across the hotel bed, he turned on the radio.

> . . . The voice of Aretha Franklin
> surprises me. I lie in the dark listening to
> black music. I think of Baldwin playing

Bessie Smith in Europe and discovering
a piece of himself inside every note.[4]

Miller, Smith, and Giovanni bear witness to the depth and reach of Aretha's archetypal soul voice. They likewise bear witness to the cultural insight and authority of that highly affective voice and its many sonic qualities. That voice and that leadership reveal a profound cultural wisdom. This is a deep knowledge, akin to that of geniuses and seers, embodied in and transmitted through her singular voice.

One night during a highly spirited mass meeting of the 1962 Albany Movement, an old Negro spiritual stately rang out:

> *Go down Moses*
> *Way down in Egypt land*
> *Tell old Pharaoh*
> *To let my people go.*

In response to this call, issued twice, another verse rang out twice, equally stately:

> *Go down Kennedy*
> *Way Down in Georgia land*
> *Tell old Pritchett*
> *To Let My People Go.[5]*

Throughout the South, "Woke Up This Morning with My Mind Stayed on Jesus" became "Woke Up This Morning with My Mind Stayed on Freedom." "We are climbing Jacob's ladder, Soldiers of the Cross" became "Do you, do you want your freedom, Soldiers of the CORE." An intensifying Black Freedom Struggle breathed new life into old lyrics.

"There could have been no Albany Movement without music," explained activist Charles Jones. "We could not have communicated with the masses of people without music. They are not articulate. But through songs, they expressed hope, suffering, even joy and love." Striking a similar note, a journalist covering the Albany Movement perceptively noted, "Some of the older Negroes in Albany came to the mass meetings at first just for the spectacle and the singing. Gradually music and the preachers won them over to the philosophy of the movement. Soon a mass involvement was being forged in the churches."[6]

"Songs a Weapon in Rights Battle: Vital New Ballads Buoy Negro Spirits across the South" heralded a *New York Times* article on August 12, 1962. As the Reverend Dr. Martin Luther King Jr. observed at the time, "The freedom songs are playing a strong and vital role in our struggle. They give the people new courage and a sense of unity. I think they keep alive a faith, a radiant hope, in the future, particularly in our most trying hours." Leaders like Fannie Lou Hamer understood the music's power. Mrs. Hamer was famous for breaking loose with a song when the spirit hit, when the need or desire arose. "This little light of mine, I'm gonna let it shine"; "Everywhere I go, I'm gonna let it shine."[7]

Black music, especially black song, spoke to needs, desires, and duties both sacred and secular. The imperatives of freedom struggle brought the sacred and the secular together, dynamically building off of each other, solidifying commitment, bracing and signifying resistance. In fact black music has both influenced and been deeply influenced by the Black Freedom Struggle. Countless times Civil Rights protestors, especially the brave youth of the Student Non-Violent Coordinating Committee, confronted vicious, often murderous, treatment and inhumane interrogations and jailings. Song helped them to endure and transcend that hell on earth. Song in this case was political practice as well as spiritual balm and psychological and emotional release.

Trying to explain how the youth of SNCC grappled with "the fear, the danger, the loneliness, the dread" of their work, in the early 1960s Howard Zinn proposed that it had something to do with the power of the music. He explained that while song had been important to other social movements,

> there has never been a singing movement like this one. Perhaps it is because most of them were brought up on gospel songs and hymns of the Negro church in the South, perhaps also because they are young, probably most of all because what they are doing inspires song. They have created a new gospel music out of the old, made up songs adapted or written in jail or on the picket line. Every battle station in the Deep South now has its Freedom Chorus, and the mass meetings there end with everyone standing, led by the youngsters of SNCC, linking arms, and singing "We Shall Overcome."

"Indeed," as Sterling Stuckey has observed of the Movement, "music backing nonviolent resistance was perhaps as powerful a means of fashioning a new day as guns have been in other places in our time."[8]

The historical centrality of black music to the black cultural matrix—to black cultural politics in particular—must be underscored. In other words, black music is an axiomatic element of black history and culture. Black music profoundly informs the larger culture's form and substance, its structure and meaning. This culture and music of both affirmation and protest signify a grand and inclusive tradition. Thus, the cultural work of "soul music," of the "Queen of Soul" Aretha Franklin, is inextricably connected to the cultural work of the "freedom songs" sung by Fannie Lou Hamer. Both express a fundamental cultural order and cultural logic: interrelated means toward a common end. Both not only helped to frame black consciousness during the modern Black Liberation Insurgency, but also thus helped to shape black thought and action. In a very real sense the music mattered precisely because the culture it came out of and represented mattered. Black cultural politics suffused and helped shape the Movement.

In the vortex of the struggle, the personal and the social were indeed political. While the Movement obviously fought over the public and the tangible, it also concerned itself with the private and interior landscapes of black people's lives. It concerned itself with the affective, the emotional, and the psychological. As the singing preachers always want to know from their audience: "How do you feel?" Part of their charge is to help people "feel" better, if only for a moment. In fact, nurturing the "soul" is absolutely vital cultural as well as social work. Like black religious music, soul music is committed to this kind of interior sustenance and uplift.

It is in this crucial yet uncharted cultural site that the work of Fannie Lou Hamer met that of Aretha Franklin: where the music and black cultural politics became one, where the divide between the sacred and the secular dissolved. Not surprisingly, given women's traditional social roles as nurturers and transmission agents for the culture, notably caretakers of its more intimate domains, they perform a great deal of this kind of cultural nurturance, notably in the family and in social networks. Generations of unheralded church mothers and community mothers, fictive kin at best, have cared deeply about and looked after the community's interests, especially its children, and thus its future. Similarly, cultural workers like Franklin and Hamer speak and sing from a perspective framed by their experiences as black women trying to make it in a world stacked against them because of their gender and race, and, more so in Hamer's case, her working-class status.

The music is of course not perfect. It too often mirrors and shapes negative features of the culture, such as sexism, homophobia, and greed. Yet this downside must be balanced against its good work. In a world too often stacked against you, the self- and group affirmation as well as the pleasure the music provides enhances the quality of life. As Robin D. G. Kelley notes, "It nonetheless helped generate community pride, challenged racial self-hatred and built self-respect. It created a world of pleasure, not just to escape the everyday brutalities of capitalism, patriarchy, and white supremacy, but to build community, establish fellowship, play and laugh, and plant seeds for a different way of living, a different way of hearing."[9] Without music, the Black Freedom Struggle, not to mention black cultural politics, would have been sorely impoverished.

Critical to the modern Black Freedom Movement was the growing African-American debate over the profound tension at the core of black identity: the duality of being at once both American and African. In his classic early twentieth-century formulation of this double consciousness, W. E. B. Du Bois vividly conceptualized it as "two warring ideals in one dark body, whose dogged strength alone keeps it from being torn asunder." Indeed, that very strength invigorated the heated debates over the dual consciousness of African Americans and the fallout from these debates during the modern Black Freedom Movement, especially in the Black Power years.

These powerful historical developments not only deeply influenced African-American culture and identity, but American culture and identity, too. Moreover, the African-American quest for both authentic historical roots—a usable past—and a viable cultural politics between 1945 and 1975 was a crucial impetus to the concurrent groundswell in what later came to be known as identity politics. This growing rediscovery and reassertion of distinctive histories by both mainstream and marginalized Americans had important consequences for American culture in the latter half of the twentieth century.

Propelled by the extraordinary example of the modern African-American Liberation Insurgency, social movements rooted in a history and culture of uncommon difference expanded among various outsiders: peoples of color (Native Americans, Latinos, Asian Americans), women, gays and lesbians, the disabled, children, and the poor. Similarly, the postwar "rise of the white ethnics" signaled an important response of insiders—white Americans—to the increasingly powerful challenge of Negroness/blackness. In fact, among innumerable white Americans, various notions of whiteness as a distinctive identity reasserted itself in both emulation of and opposition to Negroness/blackness.

The militant culture and identity of Black Power, notably its vigorous antiwhite manifestations, sparked a renewed emphasis on a dual and hyphenated white identity rooted principally in both Europe and America, such as Irish American, Polish American, German American, Italian American. This resurgent white ethnicity, notably as expressed among the suburban middle class, while largely voluntary was often shot through with ambivalence, and anxiety-ridden regarding mainstream acceptance. What Mary C. Waters labels "symbolic ethnic identity" functions largely as a choice encompassing historic roots, "authentic" cultural practices, and the satisfaction of belonging to a now accepted group. But the reality is not always all it is cracked up to be. Jews, for example, are now more fully accepted as both Jewish and American, on one hand, and as both white and American, on the other. Still antisemitism persists and all too often rears its ugly head.[10]

For peoples of color, however, especially African Americans, the intransigence of white supremacy has earmarked the postwar period. For African Americans, constraint rather than choice has continued to frame their identity options. Whereas white ethnic identities have generally ceased to be serious impediments to realization of the American Dream, the nagging persistence of racism against colored peoples still operates as a significant barrier to their full inclusion in America. Comparatively speaking, the declining impact of ethnicity stands in stark contrast to the continuing impact of race.[11]

On one level, by making the United States a better place for all Americans the modern Black Freedom Struggle clearly ameliorated the enduring dilemma of race. On another level, that insurgency exacerbated the problem of race by contributing to a white backlash, or a racist counterinsurgency, among those who saw their own status under assault as a result of black gains achieved principally through the insurgency. In this view, black progress undermined white status and white progress. In terms of black-white relations, then, the fallout from the "fury for liberty" that Vincent Harding sees as the defining mark of the postwar African-American experience has often had a downside as well as an upside.

Nowhere is this "fury for liberty" better expressed than in the wide-ranging and multifaceted African-American struggles to realize their full human potential, or the Movement. Rather than a mere fixation with Civil Rights and Black Power, the Movement wrestled with the intractable dilemma of African-American humanity in a white supremacist order. Operating within the American grain while battling against American apartheid, African Americans moved fitfully from constraint to greater choice in the construction of themselves as a people.

Clearly, the ideal of freedom in all its complexity has exerted a powerful impact on these African-American struggles for self-realization and group empowerment. In fact no ideal has exerted a greater impact on African-American history, culture, and identity. African-American popular culture—notably of the expressive variety—thus provides an illuminating window onto the Movement. Moving from slavery to emancipation, from Jim Crow to statutory equality, from stigma to respectability, African Americans have forged a history, culture, and identity smithied out of freedom's imperatives.

From the point of captivity in African communities of origin to New World black slave communities and beyond, "the great overarching movement of consciousness for Black people," building upon Stephen Henderson's argument, has been liberation, a free-dom fixation, variously understood. It is understandable, there-fore, that Robert Stepto can argue categorically and persuasively that "The quest for freedom and literacy is found in every major Afro-American text." In fact this freedom quest has been ubiqui-tous. Building upon Stepto's view, Norman Harris has provoca-tively characterized African-American freedom as "knowledge of the racial memory" and African-American literacy as "the ability to apply it."[12] These specific notions of freedom and literacy en-compass the wide range of African-American expressive culture, including dance, visual art, popular music, folklore, oral and ver-nacular genres, as well as varieties of the written text.

Nowhere is the complexity of freedom explored more artfully and powerfully than in the African-American literary tradition. Some of the most influential and inspirational African-American poetry growing out of the mid-twentieth-century African-Amer-ican "fury for liberty" bears fervent witness to the enduring vigor of these African-derived vernacular traditions of oral art. Poems like Claude McKay's 1919 "If We Must Die"—a stridently mili-tant paean to resistance during the race riots of World War I and its aftermath—heralded the self-conscious cultural emphasis on race pride and African-American militancy of the 1920s Harlem Renaissance and Marcus Garvey's Universal Negro Improvement Association. This "New Negro's" unwavering commitment to an aggressively fought freedom struggle, ironically framed in tradi-tional sonnet form, has moved untold numbers.

> If we must die, O let us nobly die,
> So that our precious blood may not be shed
> In vain; then even the monsters we defy
> Shall be constrained to honor us though dead![13]

This militant race consciousness tied to a vigilant sense of the necessity and nobility of collective race struggle clearly prefigured the mentality of the modern African-American Liberation Insurgency. A key distinction between the Harlem Renaissance and the Black Arts Renaissance of the 1960s, however, was the powerful mass social and political mobilization that fed the post–World War II movement. Though a very important mass movement in its own right, 1920s Garveyism lacked the frontal assault on Jim Crow and the integrationist ethos of the later movement. Nonetheless, at its height, Garveyism paralleled and intersected with the Harlem Renaissance and strongly encouraged a cultural nationalist emphasis on African-American pride and race unity. However, neither the Harlem Renaissance nor Garveyism produced anything among regular folk quite like the cultural politics of the midcentury mass insurgency.[14] In fact escalating black militancy during the Depression and World War II, reflecting a wide range of positions, notably leftist and radical ones, pushed the Black Freedom Struggle to its postwar explosion.

Representative of this burgeoning mid-twentieth-century African-American militancy is Margaret Walker's stirring poem "For My People." This poem has been a consistent favorite among African-American audiences since its 1942 appearance. Like "If We Must Die," it exudes a deep-seated commitment to racial pride and race struggle. This popular poem's strong message resonated especially deeply among African Americans during their Double Victory Campaign of World War II—the two-pronged offensive led by the black press against white supremacy at home and abroad. It has also been an evocative group touchstone—something akin to a "national Negro poem" or Movement poem—loudly declaimed at innumerable official and unofficial group events, large and small, since its appearance. In the construction of the official scripture of the Movement, "For My People" often worked in tandem with the national Negro anthem: "Lift Every Voice and Sing."[15] Like that song, the poem encouraged hope and relentless struggle. The last stanza pushes to a resounding climax.

Let a new earth rise. Let another world be born. Let a bloody peace
be written in the sky. Let a second generation full of courage issue
forth; let a people loving freedom come to growth. Let a beauty full
of healing and a strength of final clenching be the pulsing in our
spirits and our blood. Let the martial songs be written, let the dirges
disappear. Let a race of men now rise and take control.[16]

The powerful union of unyielding race pride and strong race unity plus unfailing commitment to liberation proved to be an increasingly popular combination during the postwar insurgency. Walker's moving call to "let a people loving freedom come to growth" soon came to pass.

The poetic marriage of race pride and undying commitment to the insurgency exemplified the increasingly assertive "New Negro" of the Civil Rights–Black Power years. Similarly, increasing attention to African-American vernacular traditions—such as music and folklore—energized the poetry. The vernacular-inflected poetry of Walker, Sterling Brown, Gwendolyn Brooks, and most notably Langston Hughes helped shape this genre. An activist vision of poetry for the people propelled the struggle. As black arts theoretician Larry Neal put it, this poetry was a vital component of a wide-ranging "art that posits for us the Vision of a Liberated Future."[17] "Black art will elevate and enlighten our people and lead them toward an awareness of self, i.e., their Blackness," explained activist poet Haki Madhubuti. "It will show them mirrors. Beautiful symbols. And will aid in the destruction of anything nasty and detrimental to our advancement as a people."[18]

In a recurrent yet significant refrain, poet Mari Evans insisted that the truth—from a black perspective—was essential to freedom. Consequently, it was absolutely imperative to "Speak Truth to the People."[19] Reflecting the dominant strain of cultural nationalism at the time, she explained that a change in consciousness was a prerequisite step toward black revolution. A free mind was essential to a free nation. Imagining and realizing such freedom—both physical and mental—was necessary to construct a viable black nation. Nation building was thus cultural as well as political, social, and economic. Nationhood, freedom, self-elevation, and community elevation were to a large measure feats of the black social imagination. That very imagination in fact fueled black collective action.

The deep-seated African-American commitment to freedom struggle has energized and pulsated throughout African-American music. Consequently, the music, especially jazz, fed off of and propelled the Movement, wittingly and unwittingly. In fact a key development in the history of jazz has been the series of innovations that seek increasingly greater freedom of artistic expression. Consequently, jazz—as a fundamentally African-American music—has served as a resonant marker of the inextricable links between the music and its context. As John Litweiler has written:

> The quest for freedom with a small f appears at the very beginning of jazz and reappears at every growing point in the music's history. The earliest jazz musicians asserted their independence of melody, structure, rhythm, and expression from the turn-of-the-century musics that surrounded them: Louis Armstrong symbolized the liberation of the late twenties jazz soloist; the Count Basie band offered liberation of jazz rhythm; and [Charlie] Parker and [Dizzy] Gillespie offered yet more new freedoms to jazz. Genuine freedom occurs when the artist can communicate most intimately with the materials, the language of his/her medium; each innovation in jazz, from the beginnings to the present, appears so that jazz artists can reveal what cannot be revealed in any other way.[20]

Indeed, the "freedom quest" in jazz has not only been pivotal to its musical evolution, but it also helps to account for its widespread international acclaim. Cultural myopia, compounded by racism, has impeded a similar recognition for jazz in the United States.

Cornel West's "jazz freedom fighters," or in Eugene Redmond's words, these "cultural warriors," personified the increasingly oppositional black cultural politics of the mid-twentieth century. These supremely gifted, popular, and committed artists pushed forward the black insurgency, specifically an oppositional black cultural politics, in several related ways. They accomplished this task through both the aggressive black cultural politics of their music and the sheer majesty and inspirational power of their work. Their virtuosity not only inspired fellow musicians and audiences; it also inspired the black social imagination to higher standards of individual excellence, social commitment, and collective action.[21]

The wartime emergence and postwar development of the jazz movement known as bebop signaled a crucial shift. Alto saxophonist Charlie Parker, trumpeter Dizzy Gillespie, pianists Thelonius Monk and Bud Powell, and drummers Kenny Clarke and Max Roach were among the African-American artists who pioneered this highly influential avant-garde idiom with its intense emotional charge; blinding tempos; complex melodies, harmonies, and chords; increased polyrhythmic urgency; and hip style. As a music, it greatly expanded the freedom of jazz improvisation. As the bebop innovators "attacked the conventional symmetry of the pop songs which underlay older jazz," writes John F. Szwed, "they expanded the role of harmony, since bop musicians were retaining and expanding the chords of the pop melodies they were eliminating." While complicating rhythm, bebop "still had a linear pulse, along with a cycle of climaxes and repeats which organized harmony and melody and which helped listeners locate themselves corporeally in the performance."[22]

As a cultural style, bebop self-consciously represented itself as a pathbreaking extension of the African-American tradition of jazz innovation. In its blatant refusal to be seen as just another form of Negro entertainment for whites, bebop captured the increasingly militant politics of the wartime and postwar "New Negro," of the Double V Campaign to defeat racism abroad and at home. Beboppers were "artists," not mere musical "entertainers." The bebop performance ethic was increasingly internally driven. The message to the audience was clear: "If you don't like it, don't listen." It was a music that plainly reflected a deep pride in distinctive African-American cultural and aesthetic traditions.

Lashing out against the history of white appropriation and theft of black musics, Monk was alleged to have said that in part bebop grew out of a concern "to create something that they can't steal because they can't play it." It was to be an in-group, or "Negro thing," reflective of Negroness, of what is represented in this discussion as black culture, as black cultural politics. Ortiz M. Walton has characterized bebop as "the beginning of a conscious black aesthetic in jazz." In fact the music's impact on jazz and American culture generally has been huge. As evidenced in the music and legend of Charlie "Bird" Parker, the greatest of the bebop players, this musical revolution tested the limits of freedom all the while inspiring a generation with a renewed and broad-gauged commitment to freedom. This liberating impact could also be seen in the fiction of Ralph Ellison, Thomas Pynchon, and Jack Kerouac. In the visual arts it could be seen among Abstract Expressionists like Romare Bearden, Larry Rivers, and Jackson Pollock. It likewise deeply influenced a disparate array of poets, comedians, and performance artists often lumped together as the "cools," "the beats," "the hipsters," "beatniks," including poets Alan Ginsberg and Bob Kaufmann and comedian Lenny Bruce.[23]

The landmark 1954 *Brown* decision outlawing Jim Crow in public school education and the catalytic Montgomery bus boycott (1955–56) fanned the flames of black cultural politics. One concurrent development, in part an expression of black cultural politics, was a variety of bop ironically termed hard bop. This was a jazz style that was more popular and commercially viable than its often more technically challenging immediate predecessor. Like the *Brown* decision and the Montgomery bus boycott, hard bop marked a shift in African-American consciousness. Hard bop married bebop with vernacular genres, including down-home blues (rural-based, gritty, earthy); the more urbane, or citified, rhythm and blues; and gospel. As with vernacular-inflected poetry, vernacular-inflected hard bop was a big hit. Often labeled "soul jazz," this music, like 1960s soul music, was both earthier and more church-based than the original.

Drummer Art Blakey, pianist Horace Silver, organist Jimmy Smith, guitarist Wes Montgomery, and alto saxophonist Julian "Cannonball" Adderley helped to spearhead this unabashedly popular music. Besides "a return to the pulsing rhythms and earthy emotions of jazz's 'roots,'" according to David Rosenthal, it encompassed several trends. One was an engagement with popular black traditions, as in Jimmy Smith's urban-blues-influenced "Midnight Special." Another was the "more astringent," "starker and more tormented," "somber," "sometimes tragic" music of saxophonists like Tina Brooks and pianists like Mal Waldron. It also included "a gentler, more lyrical bent," evident in the work of musicians like pianist Hank Jones and trumpeter Art Farmer. Finally, again in Rosenthal's formulation, it would include a range of jazz experimentalists such as bassist and composer extraordinaire Charles Mingus, whose work overlapped with previous styles, forged new ones, and foreshadowed others to come.[24]

Like Mingus' "Wednesday Night Prayer Meeting" and his "Prayer for Passive Resistance," this was a music that spoke far more affirmatively and directly than bebop to the immediate, everyday world of the postwar African-American "fury for liberty." As evident in other contemporary forms of African-American popular culture, including the visual arts, hard bop celebrated an accessible, open, and flexible freedom. As with comparable forms of black expressive culture, like gospel and rhythm and blues, hard bop also contributed to the store of psychic and cultural energies demanded by the intensifying social struggle. The soulful cultural politics of hard bop thus revealed the increasingly assertive Negro consciousness of the escalating Civil Rights Movement.[25]

That freedom remained a central theme of black cultural politics is evident in the principal developments of jazz during the 1960s and early 1970s: free jazz and jazz fusion (a jazz marriage with rock, soul, and pop musics). Much has been made, however, of the fact that after 1930s swing, jazz has declined as a truly popular music, especially since the postwar upsurge of rock and roll. From its height of popularity during the Depression, when it was America's most popular music, it has been displaced in popularity by a variety of rock-and-roll, dance-based, genres. Bebop was neither dance music nor a crowd pleaser, while an important element of hard bop recaptured danceabilty and restored some of jazz's dwindling market share.

Precisely because of its independence from considerations of mass-market popularity, a significant element of the jazz of the Civil Rights–Black Power era interacted even more directly with the Movement. Marketing concerns and crossover dreams—the hope of hits going beyond the black market and capturing the larger and far more lucrative white one—inhibited the more popular black musics, notably rhythm and blues and soul, from a fuller and comparable engagement with the insurgency. These artists, producers, and executives did not want to alienate potential white customers; and this perspective reinforced the integrationist thrust of the Civil Rights years.[26]

The Black Power years saw more and more attention to the liberation struggle in rhythm and blues, and soul music in particular. Yet in many ways the most powerful and uncompromising musical statements on behalf of the Black Liberation Insurgency came out of 1960s jazz. The work of highly political jazz artists like Max Roach, whose 1960 recording of the important *Freedom Now*

Suite, featuring the haunting vocals of Abbey Lincoln (Aminata Moseka), directly engaged the struggle. With its striking jazz commentaries on slavery ("Driva' Man"), emancipation ("Freedom Day"), and the expanding Civil Rights Movement ("Tryptich: Prayer/Protest/Peace"), its cultural politics were deeply historical, radical, and activist.[27]

Freedom Now Suite epitomized the charged and expectant mood of the times. The sit-in movement was in full swing. Reflecting the burgeoning internationalist and pan-African point of view within the movement, the album emphasized the ties of the African-American Liberation Insurgency to the many liberation struggles on the African continent ("All Africa"), especially the growing grassroots insurgency against the South African apartheid system ("Tears for Johannesburg"). In sum, the project was a powerful statement on behalf of human freedom.[28]

In its comparable engagement with the Black Freedom Struggle, free jazz, exemplified by the *Freedom Now Suite,* projected a militant black cultural politics. "Free jazz" is the label attached to the post-bop musical revolution spearheaded not only by saxophonist John Coltrane, but also by contemporary musicians like multi-instrumentalist Eric Dolphy, pianist Cecil Taylor, and, most important, saxophonist Ornette Coleman. Earlier work like the atonal music of pianist Sun Ra and bassist Charles Mingus as well as the chordless music of Coleman and Taylor foreshadowed free jazz.

It was the iconoclastic Coleman who threw down the free jazz gauntlet. In 1958 he explained: "I think one day music will be a lot freer. Then the pattern for a tune . . . will be forgotten and the tune itself will be the pattern, and won't have to be forced into conventional patterns. The creation of music is just as natural as the air we breathe. I believe music is really a free thing, and any way you can enjoy it you should."[29] This expansive musical vision paralleled much of what was happening in classical music at the time, and in both reflected a noteworthy degree of cross-fertilization.[30] This at times seemingly boundless sense of freedom struck some critics as rudderless music. For proponents, however, it was a revelation.

Free jazz nonetheless tended to operate within certain parameters. It typically was not wholly without a sense of structure and direction. Six defining features of free jazz, according to Len Lyons, are:

> (a) the liberation of melody from preset chord changes and fixed tempo; (b) the creation of new song structures, some of which resemble modern classical music more than blues or ballads; (c) the creation of sound surfaces by the use of tonal coloration; (d) the creation of sound fields by the use of instrumental density and coloration; (e) the use of new or uncommon instruments—and new uses of traditional instruments—to further (c) and (d); and (f) group improvisation, composition, and overall interaction (collectivism), revising the previously dominant role of the soloist.[31]

These parameters clearly opened up the music dramatically, greatly expanding the freedom of jazz improvisation.

The strikingly original music of Coleman and other free jazz players, like that of Parker and his bebop comrades, was highly virtuosic and challenging. Not surprisingly, the avant-garde artistry of free jazz failed to impress many at the time. In fact, not unlike bebop, free jazz met critical and popular controversy as well as limited sales. Nevertheless, the tremendous expansion of the emancipatory ethos of the music was a significant achievement. What Litweiler has posited of Coleman's music and its influence applies to the major free jazz players. Coleman's "liberation of jazz melody from traditional fetters of harmonic and rhythmic patterns," Litweiler maintains, "certainly resulted in genuine freedom of expression for his own music." And, as he further explains, it "implied similar freedom to the generations that followed." Here he refers principally to future generations of musicians. Yet the point has animated the expanding freedom ethos of modern black cultural politics, on one side, and the inter-related Civil Rights–Black Power and post–Black Power Movements, on the other.[32]

In roughly the final decade of his life, the legendary and extraordinarily influential John Coltrane exuded a "fury for liberty." In short order, in the early 1960s he became the most popular of the free jazz explorers and quickly achieved the greatest acclaim within the idiom and among innumerable fans. Although Coltrane was not as openly political as artists like Max Roach and tenor saxophonist Archie Shepp, a Coltrane protégé, many see him, among other things, as the cultural personification of the modern African-American "freedom quest." Countless numbers have experienced and thus represented his music and his life struggle as liberatory.

A large portion of his most influential music is profoundly spiritual, reflecting his wide-ranging interests in world musics and world religions. Consequently, many view his music as a special medium for the achievement of enlightenment of spiritual, personal, and collective varieties. Indeed, many agree with Eric Nisenson, who argues that it is precisely because of Coltrane's musical "pursuit of God—his great quest—that Coltrane's music has the ineffable charisma that continues to fascinate so many." This spiritual adulation of Coltrane and the related and godlike representations of him perhaps say more about others and their needs and projections than about Coltrane the musician and artist. As Francis Davis has argued, "More than any other performer of his time or ours, he is a god we create, if not in our own image, then according to our desires and beliefs."[33]

Easily the most gripping example of a spiritual vision of Coltrane's music is San Francisco's fiery, Pentecostalist-influenced Saint John Coltrane Will-I-Am African Orthodox Church. For more than thirty years this church has featured a fervent musical and religious experience and honored Coltrane as its patron saint.

In an ecstatic, at times overpowering, worship service cum jazz concert, a truly hybrid ritual affair, members and visitors alike are challenged to plumb the spiritual depths of Coltrane's music and persona. In addition to the resident drums, saxophones, and trumpets, the congregants—members and visitors alike—are encouraged to play their own instruments, or to participate by playing a tambourine or other percussive instruments, given out as one enters the house of worship. Taking very seriously the biblical injunction to "make a joyful noise unto the Lord," the congregants are invited to clap, stomp, and shout, in other words, to invoke and celebrate the spirit.[34]

Coltrane's phoenixlike rise from the wasteland of drugs to the promised land of an intertwined musical and spiritual enlightenment has thus proven enormously inspirational. After his spiritual epiphany and newfound dedication to clean living, his music grew by leaps and bounds. Like other iconic figures in jazz—such as "Bird" (Charlie Parker)—"Trane" soon assumed a larger-than-life persona that has only grown since his untimely death at age forty in 1967. In his lifetime, he was deeply influenced by the African-American Freedom Struggle: witness his "Alabama"—an achingly beautiful tribute to the four African-American girls killed in the September 1963 bombing of Birmingham's Sixteenth Street Baptist Church. As Coltrane himself explained, the song "represents, musically, something that I saw down there translated into music from inside me."[35]

In spite of his relative public quiescence, however, many within and outside the movement saw his music as representative of the volcanic shifts in experience and consciousness that African Americans were enduring in their "freedom quest." His widespread musical influence derived from various achievements, including, as Lyons has written, "(1) his tone and technique on the soprano and alto saxes; (2) his lengthy, developmental modal, or scalar, improvising; and (3) his wholehearted dedication to music as a moral and spiritual force." It is not surprising, therefore, especially in light of his own profoundly spiritual view of his music, that for innumerable African Americans and others, Coltrane became a symbol par excellence of black cultural politics as shaped by the emerging black consciousness and the escalating Black Freedom Struggle.[36]

The huge number of black poems that grapple with "Trane" and his passionate music tell us a great deal about his enormous influence, not simply as a jazz musician but as an exemplar of improvisatory greatness and blackness. One critic has hazarded that there are more poems about Coltrane than any other jazz musician. In "Dear John, Dear Coltrane," poet Michael Harper employs the call-and-response framework so fundamental to African-American culture and invokes the spiritual, worldly, and evocative qualities that infused Coltrane's music. Repeating the mesmerizing refrain from Coltrane's most famous composition, "A Love Supreme," the poem achieves a rhythmic and incantatory tension offset by its rich vernacular backbeat.

> *a love supreme*
> *a love supreme . . .*
>
> *Why you so black?*
> *cause I am*
> *Why you so funky?*
> *cause I am*
> *Why you so black?*
> *cause I am*
> *Why you so sweet?*
> *cause I am*
> *Why you so black?*
> *cause I am*
> *a love supreme, a love supreme.*[37]

In the realm of popular music, the soul idiom unleashed a furious assault on behalf of freedom. Culturally and psychologically speaking, soul music achieved its unrivaled emotional power principally from its vernacular roots in the blues and gospel. The most intense expressions of soul music—as exemplified in the music of Ray Charles, James Brown, Etta James, and Otis Redding—shattered the secular-sacred divide, reveling in the charged aftermath. The marriage of the Black Freedom Struggle to soul music was a highly spirited union and gave popular currency to varieties of black cultural politics. In a very real sense, this often viscerally keen music was a deep meditation on "the Southern dream of freedom," as Peter Guralnick illustrates in *Sweet Soul Music.* "It represents," he explains, "another chapter in the development of black consciousness, similar to the Harlem Renaissance, say, in its championing of negritude, but more widespread in its immediate impact."[38]

In 1967, when "Soul Sister Number One" Aretha Franklin demanded "Respect," everyone took notice. Redolent of the audacious public posture of the Black Panther Party for Self-Defense that was achieving notoriety at the same time, the Queen of Soul's powerful demand heralded an increasingly assertive black self. With her stunning voice, this Memphis-born daughter of the famous preaching and gospel-singing phenomenon Dr. C. L. Franklin became an even greater cultural phenomenon. Artfully combining and reworking a variety of musical genres, she took whatever she sang to another level, drenching it with an incomparable gospel blues style. When she shouted "Think," the glorious gospel-inflected refrain of "Freedom" stirred deeply felt and roiling emotions.[39]

Aretha "is undoubtedly the one person who put everyone on notice," discerned Nikki Giovanni in her "Poem for Aretha." It was Aretha who "pushed every Black singer into Blackness and negro entertainers into negroness." Indeed, "there has been no musician whom her very presence hasn't affected." Because of Aretha, Giovanni concluded:

> the Black songs started coming from the singers on stage
>   and the dancers
> in the streets.[40]

Soul music flowered between 1966 and 1975, alongside the Black Power Insurgency. For Guralnick and countless others, "soul music was black power . . . a kind of revolutionary statement of purpose, a bold departure from the rhythm and blues which preceded it." Soul music was Negroes coming into an appreciation of their blackness, achieving a qualitative and quantitative shift in black consciousness. This expanding black consciousness signified black commitment to the struggle. That consciousness likewise signified both a new and revitalized black cultural politics, or, as William Van Deburg illustrates, a "new day in Babylon."[41]

Nina Simone, the "High Priestess of Soul," personified this militant black cultural politics and set a benchmark for black music of protest and affirmation. In a wide-ranging and influential body of work, running from her spare yet highly evocative vignettes of black women's lives in "Four Women," to her caustic satire on southern apartheid, "Mississippi Goddamn," she energized soul music and black cultural politics. The even more popular Impressions, featuring Curtis Mayfield, similarly promoted the escalating cultural politics of the African-American Freedom Struggle with hits like "People Get Ready," "We're a Winner," and "Keep on Pushin'." Soul fired the poetry, and vice versa. In "Revolutionary Music," Giovanni explained that

> *we be digging all*
> *our revolutionary music consciously or un*
> *cause Sam Cooke said "a change is gonna come."*[42]

Artists like Nina Simone, the Impressions, Aretha Franklin, and James Brown were "soul freedom fighters," calling to mind Cornel West's "jazz freedom fighters." Their exceptional body of work and their integrated aesthetic and political sensibility drew inspiration from, and in turn inspired, the Movement. These "soul freedom fighters" likewise personified Askia Muhammad

Toure's characterization of these kinds of artists as key "poet philosophers" of the Movement.[43] These "poet-philosophers," to reprise a popular dictum of the times, spoke the "truth" to the people in the hope of pushing forward black awareness and advancing black collective action.

Perhaps no artist better personified the "soul freedom fighter" than James Brown, "Soul Brother Number One." Amiri Baraka, the most influential cultural nationalist of the day and, among other achievements, a major and influential poet in his own right, called James Brown "our no. 1 black poet."[44] In crucial ways, the pathbreaking work of "The Godfather of Soul" during the Civil Rights–Black Power Insurgency spoke tellingly to popular expressions of black cultural politics. Brown's fascinating body of work proved especially important to raging discussions at the time of a black aesthetic, especially to notions of what is distinctive about black culture, black aesthetics, black style.

"If there is any man who symbolizes the vast differences between black and white cultural and aesthetic values, Soul Brother No. 1 (along with Ray Charles) is that man," observed David Levering Lewis. "JB was proof that black people were different," noted Thulani Davis. "Rhythmically and tonally blacks had to be from somewhere else. Proof that Africa was really over there for those of us who had never seen it—it was in that voice." Mel Watkins maintained: "As an artist and entertainer, James Brown is the personification of blackness, the embodiment of the black life style. His significance lies in his fidelity to that life style and his deft evocation of its nuances and subtleties." In a poem titled "In the Funk World," Baraka summed it up nicely: If Elvis Presley was the "King," James Brown had to be "God."[45]

"Soul Brother Number One" picked up on the Black Power vibe and connected it to a propulsive African-derived polyrhythmic attack and dense sonic universe that literally commanded listeners to dance and to have a good time. With black popular dance providing a source of pleasure and psychic release central to black life and black cultural politics at the time, Brown's incomparable dance grooves proved indispensable. A serious dance party without the latest groove from "Soul Brother Number One" was impossible.

A highly innovative and charismatic performer, the self-styled "hardest-working man in show business" put on a deftly packaged yet stunning spectacle. It artfully combined well-honed black performance techniques with black preacherly effects. The tight-knit band and earthy backup singers performed with amazing verve and efficiency. Instrumentals, vocals, and choreography made up a seamless whole. Everybody on the stage was dressed to impress. By the time of Brown's dramatic entrance, the audience was already worked up into a frenzy. He just took the frenzy to higher and higher levels.

With his own slick, acrobatic dance moves, a well-paced mix of up-tempo and slow tunes, and a dramatic conclusion where he got so worked up that he literally could not be removed from the stage, "Soul Brother Number One" mesmerized audiences. After seeing Brown at one of his typically fantastic concerts at Harlem's Apollo Theater, the central stage in popular black performance history, an anonymous black teenager marveled at Brown's trend-setting showmanship. Seeing the show as representative of Brown's authentic blackness rather than the carefully choreographed spectacle that it was, the overwrought teenager explained: "The dude is as down as a chitlin."[46]

During the height of the Black Power Insurgency, "Soul Brother Number One" demanded that his people act upon the "Black is beautiful" imperative. He implored them to "Say It Loud—I'm Black And I'm Proud!" In "I Don't Want Nobody to Give Me Nothing (Open Up the Door I'll Get It Myself)," he jammed to the imperative of black self-determination. He blasted the bombast of far too many so-called leaders in "Talkin' Loud and Sayin' Nothing." His "Get Up, Get into It and Get Involved" worked the theme of individual commitment to collective action.

And "Soul Power" energetically paraphrased the black political rallying cry for Black Power.[47]

Brown personified the American Dream, rising from poverty and incarceration to wealth and fame. He personified a kind of larger-than-life black success. As Nelson George has observed, "Motown may have been the sound of young America, but Brown was clearly the king of black America." Yet even "black royalty," notably Brown, was by no means infallible. His endorsement of Richard Nixon in the 1972 presidential election proved to be a major miscalculation. Late in the campaign Brown gave his support to the president because of his emphasis on black capitalism as a variety of black power and Brown's belief that Nixon was unbeatable. As a result of his support of Nixon, Soul Brother Number One endured withering black criticism and a significant loss in credibility among many.[48]

Brown's heavily rhythm-drenched and sonically complex explorations laid the necessary groundwork for the late 1960s emergence of funk music: a wide umbrella covering a diversity of styles unified by the "The One," the universal beat, in its infinite variations. Guitarist Jimi Hendrix, Sly and the Family Stone, and Funkadelic, featuring George Clinton, epitomized this efflorescence of popular black musical freedom. Not unlike previous black musics, funk found inspiration in and to an extent pushed forward both the black social imagination and black cultural politics. It also fed off of a number of the concurrent social struggles, such as opposition to the Vietnam war.

The popular Sly and the Family Stone demanded that you had to take a "Stand!" They also assured their audience that "You Can Make It If You Try." Finally, in "Thank You for Talkin' to Me Africa," they gave witness to the music's pan-African connection, an Afrodiasporic culture, and the freedom struggle's indebtedness to that root culture. The point was to use Black Power cultural politics as a springboard for larger visions and actions. Physical liberation necessitated mental liberation, as black cultural nationalist theoreticians intoned. Funkadelic put the fundamental challenge of their freedom ethos animating "The Funk" squarely on the line in the title tune of their second album, "Free Your Mind and Your Ass Will Follow."[49] In other words, consciousness necessarily informed action.

Funk, according to Rickey Vincent, is "the successor to the soul music of the 1960s in terms of its representations of popular black values—particularly those ideals of social, spiritual, and political redemption." Its breadth as well as its depth has enhanced its enduring power and resiliency.

> Funk music combines aspects of a wide range of black musical traditions. The blues, rhythm and blues, soul music, progressive jazz, African percussion, psychedelics, and synthesizers all find a place in the rich structure of The Funk. Funk music is a direct offspring of the blues in terms of its intimacy, intensity, and meaning for "common" black folks in the decade of integration [and beyond]. Funk music, with its nonstop, sweaty dance appeal, is also the no-nonsense form of dance entertainment most directly related to the rhythm and blues tradition. Good, loud dance music has always been the antidote to black America's troubles, and The Funk has served this purpose admirably.[50]

Jimi Hendrix's contribution to the advance of "The Funk" worked in two mutually enriching directions. His music was richly hybrid. Hendrix liberated the blues through an infusion of original and influential electric guitar work. Similarly, he liberated rock through an equally influential infusion of rhythm and blues. Many blacks at the time found his music entirely too free and, according to their soulful sonic universe, too beholden to allegedly "white" forms of rock music.

Hendrix pushed those even more deeply embedded in the soul idiom than himself, like Sly Stone and George Clinton, to expand their use of cutting-edge electronics and rock influences. Showcasing his original, hybridized musical aesthetic beyond the formal strictures of both the blues and rock, his famous funk rock version of the "Star-Spangled Banner" at the celebrated Woodstock Festival in 1969 stretched that tune to the breaking point.[51] Hendrix's work thus exemplifies the musical cross-pollination and improvisatory genius seen in the best of African-American expressive culture, especially the music. It also speaks to the complex racial politics, notably the mixed roots, of the culture and its music. Most important, Hendrix's work is a revealing demonstration of how his people's freedom struggle and the larger freedom ethos of the times intersected. His death from a drug overdose before reaching age thirty spoke volumes about the perils of freedom's excesses. His death also spoke volumes about the intense pressures of black success in a white supremacist environment.

Perhaps nowhere is the complexity of post–World War II black cultural politics better glimpsed than in the eclectic music and persona of the incomparable Sun Ra. Birmingham-born Herman Poole "Sonny" Blount was a complicated individual who luxuriated in the American tradition of self-invention throughout his music and his life. Artistically and personally, Sun Ra exemplified freedom as restraint as well as freedom as liberation. As an innovative "jazz freedom fighter," he was deeply committed to opening up new vistas of the freedom struggle. His work as a "jazz freedom fighter" enriched his work as a serious and compelling jazz intellectual, and vice versa.[52] For him the music was omnivocal, not merely polyvocal. The black social imagination opened outward not only to a global culture, but to an extraterrestrial consciousness. Paradoxically, he was truly both "out there" and firmly rooted in the here and now.

The mature Sun Ra often explained that while freedom was certainly desirable, true earthly freedom was an illusion, a trick. True freedom, he explained, looked outward from the earth toward the spiritual, the otherworldly, and the cosmic. Following upon his careful crafting of an intriguing identity as an extraterrestrial traveler looking down on the foibles of mere humanity, Sun Ra's dense musical, cultural, and historical ideas were nothing if not ambiguous and at times opaque. That very ambiguity and opacity, however, shrouds a telling commentary on the meanings and limits of human freedom, variously conceived and practiced. Freedom, Sun Ra consistently maintained, was a seductive yet woefully misunderstood and most imperfectly practiced human ideal.[53]

Sun Ra pioneered the space travel concept in jazz expressly and modern African-American popular culture more generally as an expression of the enduring African-American freedom quest. "Space is the place," he argued, where true freedom was to be realized. Indeed, throughout the African-American experience, freedom of movement—social, political, economic, cultural, and intellectual, as well as physical—has been a vital aspect of the liberation struggle. From the beginning, slaves ran away to freedom within the slave South and across the Mason-Dixon line to the "free" North. Upon emancipation, they moved around extensively, largely within the South, as a way to test out their newly won liberty. In the twentieth century, well over a million African Americans moved north during World War I, and millions more moved north and west during World War II. All of this movement was integral to their search for true freedom.

Sun Ra's cosmic search for the ultimate meaning of liberty is an elaboration of the African-American expression of a world-historical phenomenon: human movement in search of freedom. Crucial aspects of the African-American example of this global migratory pattern in the twentieth century have been urbanization—movement from the country to the city—and industrialization—movement from the farm to the factory. In effect, the African-American Freedom Struggle continues to embody a people moving en masse toward their spiritual, psychological, emotional, and physical freedom. It was precisely this kind of multilayered freedom that the cultural politics of Sun Ra explored.

The music itself is an intoxicating brew of the traditional (swing, boogie-woogie, blues) and the avant-garde (bop, free jazz, and beyond) with a heavy overlay of cosmic consciousness filtered through an African-American purview. The talented musicians are often multi-instrumentalists. As leader of various incarnations of the Intergalactic Arkestra, Sun Ra directed an unusually exciting big band whose spectacular style riveted audiences, typically commanding their active participation, not just their rapt attention. Participation might run to clapping, foot stomping, shouts, even dancing. A sensuous spirituality earmarked the band's performative identity as well as its aesthetic vision. Elaborate costumes, dancers, film and video projections of ancient Egytian motifs and space themes, incense and smoke, processions, and chants all enhanced the mix. Most important, extraordinary music keyed the experience. This compelling extravaganza thus artfully combined mythic consciousness and showmanship with first-rate musical artistry. The show in turn established an unrivaled and influential standard for African-American music as a performance art.

To the uninitiated, a performance by Sun Ra's troupe might appear to be freedom run amok. In actuality it was a highly structured and evocative improvisation playing joyfully with the tension between control and freedom. In the context of the cultural politics of the African-American Freedom Insurgency, Sun Ra stood both at its center—in his unwavering commitment to freedom—and apart—in his refusal to be sidetracked by mere earthly concerns. His was a truly cosmic angle on the freedom struggle.[54]

Perceived by many as an eccentric maverick, Sun Ra nonetheless played to enthusiastic if not always large audiences. He fearlessly forged ahead, far more concerned with advancing his admittedly idiosyncratic cultural politics than with achieving mass popularity, which in fact eluded him. As such, his visionary liberation quest relentlessly and consistently interrogated the received wisdom of freedom as a unitary, progressive, and clear-cut human condition. In his worldview, freedom was fragmented, multidirectional, and ambiguous.

Sun Ra's understanding of the allusive, elusive, and ambiguous dimensions of freedom derived from a deep acquaintance with history, especially that of African Americans. In the nineteenth century, the "quasi-freedom" of free blacks—an antebellum twilight zone between black slavery and white freedom—seriously distorted early American democracy. Similarly, the severe repression of African Americans in the aftermath of emancipation and the Civil War in the 1860s raised the question: "How free was free?" A southern white contemporary who saw the extreme restrictions against African-American freedom as fully consistent with their newfound emancipation explained that the ex-slaves had been guaranteed "nothing but freedom." A hundred years later, at the height of the Black Liberation Insurgency, Nina Simone sang movingly of this enduring dilemma in her popular version of Dr. Billy Taylor's "I Wish I Knew How It Would Feel to Be Free."[55]

These historical judgments are obviously much more than mere rhetorical laments. As evident in Sun Ra's critique, pointed perceptions about the complexities and harsh realities of freedom go to the heart of the dilemma. These understandings speak powerfully to the recognition that the very nature and reality of freedom are fundamentally paradoxical: palpable yet mysterious, knowable yet unfathomable. As Sun Ra and many others have persistently argued, the pernicious yet powerful myth of race structured a central dilemma of American freedom: a white freedom forged in the foundry of black slavery. As a result, the enduring impact of freedom's paradox, compounded by race, made the postwar African-American Freedom Insurgency all the more challenging.

The freedom quest of Sun Ra was cosmic and singular, and

thus less directly influential on the Movement. In contrast, the influence on the freedom quest of African-American religion has been deep and pervasive. As illustrated in the Movement's spiritual nexus, the psychic and emotional catharsis of African-American religion has been critical to African-American history and culture. Typically within this religious worldview, the Movement has been seen as part of God's plan for the uplift of the race. As the music of "good news in bad times," to paraphrase the subtitle of Tony Heilbut's classic discussion of the music, gospel has helped sustain belief in African-American deliverance on earth as well as in heaven.[56] In effect, by merging the struggles for earthly freedom and heavenly peace, African-American religiosity, as showcased in gospel music, buttressed the consciousness of struggle, endurance, and transcendence so vital to the emerging wartime and postwar activist ethos. It contributed mightily to the steadfast resistance and hope characteristic of the modern black social imagination and black cultural politics.

It might appear that gospel is the least political and worldly of African-American musics. In fact the opposite is true. Gospel music—like the spirituals—is highly political in a broad sense of the term, if for no other reason than that it functions as a means to constitute a unified community, to forge a collective consciousness. It likewise functions as a locus of unrestrained celebration as well as a soothing balm. It offers hope and possibility. As with the spirituals, the fundamental concerns are the eminently worldly ones of affirmation and joy. Resignation, defeat, and melancholy are for the weak and faint of heart, not for those confirmed in the faith, not to mention those baptized in the struggle. A robustly optimistic, modern sacral music, with a "good beat," gospel draws selectively from other African-American musics—notably the spirituals, blues, and rhythm and blues—in spite of its often traditional theological setting. Gospel is thus infectiously insistent in its assertion that spiritual freedom is intimately tied to the here and now, to earthly freedom.[57]

Like the impress of African-American culture on American culture, that of gospel on American culture, especially popular culture, is only dimly perceived. Nevertheless, it is significant, particularly in its impact on American and global music. Glorious solo and group voices, among the best to be heard, have influenced countless others in secular as well as sacred music. The improvisational vocal flair of the likes of Clara Ward, Inez Andrews, Marion Williams, Roberta Martin, Edna Gallmon Cooke, Queen C. Anderson, Ira Tucker, R. H. Harris, Archie Brownlee, Joe May, Claude Jeter, and the "Queen of Gospel" Mahalia Jackson often pushed the audience to the limits—and beyond—of spiritual ecstasy: in other words, "bringing down the house."

Soul music was not the only salient offshoot of gospel's grappling with "honesty of emotion," a critical marker of the wide-ranging freedom of expression characterizing each genre. Tony Heilbut explains that a kind of "authentic" soul music has reigned in gospel precisely because "church people understand spirit, 'soul' if you will, better than anyone." One staunch "saint" argued strenuously for the superiority of gospel to soul as a more spiritually and emotionally authentic music. "After all, we invented it. All this mess you hear calling itself soul ain't nothing but warmed-over gospel."[58]

Gospel's impact on the broader cultural matrix is unmistakable. It ranges widely across expressive culture—notably music, theater, and dance—and infuses the freedom songs of the modern African-American Liberation Insurgency. African-American religiosity, spirituality if you prefer, is where the black collective imagination is continuously reiterated, revitalized, expanded, and remade. The impact on black cultural politics as well as black movement culture is deep and powerful. The stereotypical church scene in popular cultural representations of African-American religious life seeks to tap into this terrain. In effect, it exploits the unrestrained freedom and deep power associated with African-American spirituality, the cultural politics of gospel in particular. Regarding rock music generally, Heilbut perceptively argues that its

> most resilient features, the beat, the drama, the group vibrations derive from gospel. From rock symphonies to detergent commercials, from Aretha Franklin's awesome feeling and technique to the Beatles' harmonies, gospel has simply reformed our listening expectations. The very tension between beats, the climax we anticipate almost subliminally, is straight out of church. The dance steps that ushered in a new physical freedom copied from the shout, the holy dance of "victory." The sit-ins soothed by hymns, the freedom marches powered by shouts, the "brother" and "sister" fraternity of revolution: the gospel church gave us all these.[59]

From the voter registration drives of the 1940s and 1950s, to the Montgomery bus boycott in the mid-1950s, to the Poor People's March in 1968, to the campaigns to elect black officials in the 1970s, and beyond, freedom songs sustained faith, courage, and unity among African Americans. In fact freedom songs have been a central feature of the African-American experience from the beginning. During the modern African-American Freedom Insurgency, spirituals, hymns, and gospel music energized mass meetings in African-American churches and innumerable private as well as public venues of struggle, notably marches, boycotts, picket lines, sit-ins, and freedom rides. Imprisoned activists often kept up their hopes by singing freedom songs.

Rhythm and blues, soul, and funk music often energized the more secular arenas of the struggle in offices, on streetcorners, in barbershops and beauty parlors, in parks and on playgrounds, and in social affairs. Wherever people congregated, sacred, secular, and hybrid song was a key element in the daily ritual of liberation struggle. Bernice Johnson Reagon has spoken of "the songs as the language that focused the energy of the people who filled the streets and roads of the South." The widespread cross-fertilization of songs and messages—"Get Your Rights, Jack," sung to the punchy piano riff of Ray Charles's "Hit the Road Jack"; or Aretha's dramatic, gospel-inflected "To Be Young, Gifted, and Black"—effectively bridged the sacred-secular divide, broadening the music's appeal.[60]

In many ways, the most soulful and empowering music of the struggle came out of African-American religious traditions: not just the more traditional forms of sacred music—spirituals and hymns—which made up much of the extraordinary body of Movement freedom songs, but also the more contemporaneous, less-understood, and thus less-appreciated gospel tunes. The large and small ways in which gospel, like African-American religion and music generally, has historically steeled African-American faith and determination, wittingly and unwittingly, can be neither quantified nor underestimated. While atypical, direct commentary on the contemporary social struggle was certainly not unheard of, especially in innumerable concerts, worship services, and meetings where the spirit took control and the problems of African Americans cried out for an improvised interpolation. Not surprisingly, therefore, in 1942 the Golden Gate Quartet sang of "No Segregation in Heaven." Similarly, in the 1950s Dorothy Love Coates and Reverend Julius Cheeks, the "Queen and King" of the "Gospel Highway"—the popular gospel concert circuit—spoke out forcefully against the racism and injustice bedeviling their people. They carried the southern-based African-American freedom struggle wherever they went.[61]

Most gospel music, however, dealt first and foremost with fundamentally spiritual concerns—the notion of the soul's salvation—in a musical form, as Heilbut so aptly puts it, "with almost unlimited artistic freedoms." It is that expansively liberating musical and sacred universe which resonated most deeply with and undergirded the Movement. When Mahalia Jackson sang "Move

On Up a Little Higher," the message exuded support for the freedom struggle as well as for living righteously in order to make it to heaven. Similarly, in 1963, when the Caravans, featuring Shirley Caesar, exhorted that God neither wanted, needed, nor tolerated a "Coward Soldier" in "His Band," the meaning for the Movement was compelling. As Caesar and the Caravans so resolutely proclaimed in their rousing "No Coward Soldier": "when the children of God get together, they're sure gonna rock the nation!"[62] These and kindred foot soldiers were indeed indispensable to the grassroots insurgency that threw up the charismatic generalship of the Reverend Dr. Martin Luther King Jr.

America, indeed the world, has never been the same.

CHAPTER 3

"Be Real Black for Me"

Embodying and Representing Blackness

HOW DOES BLACKNESS come to be embodied literally and figuratively, actually as well as symbolically? In his classic autobiography, *Up from Slavery,* Booker T. Washington spoke of the former slaves like himself struggling to make it clear that the "freedom in their songs meant freedom of the body in this world."[1] Those songs of course were not only musical ones, but also cultural expressions representative of black artistic and aesthetic endeavors more broadly. They were metaphorical songs, "sung" in fields as diverse yet related as sports and visual arts. The artists and cultural workers treated here demonstrate that the "fury for liberty" so fundamental to their work represents the ongoing black battle for an expansive vision of corporeal freedom, an unfettered "freedom of the body" in this world. Ultimately, this is a paradoxical freedom: a freedom at once bounded and unbounded by race.

As a guiding theory and practice, a "fury for liberty" frames the cultural politics of the modern Black Insurgency, particularly expressive realms like sports, dance, and visual arts. That freedom quest has been inseparably aesthetic and political, both propelling and propelled by the ongoing African-American Freedom Struggle. A definitive challenge throughout has been remaking the American nation and the interrelated African-American nation so that both nations fully recognize and vigorously extend their intrinsic blackness. Recasting American culture from an African-American cultural point of view has thus been a crucial element of the modern Black Freedom Struggle, especially the Black Arts Movement and the more inclusive domain of black cultural politics.

The postwar American sports scene has undergone a transformative African-American infusion. In the popular sports worlds of boxing, baseball, and football, the impact of black athletes and identifiably black cultural styles has been profound. Nowhere has this impact been more pronounced than in professional basketball. By the latter third of the twentieth century, "America's game" had become a quintessentially African-American field of endeavor. The pivotal shift from professional basketball as a white sport to a black one transpired alongside of, and was in some measure a consequence of, the triumph of the Civil Rights–Black Power Movement.

Nowhere has the color line in the major professional sports fallen so completely as in basketball. The improvisational flair and aesthetic virtuosity so central to African-American culture have been on abundant display in the National Basketball Association since the 1960s with the arrival of significant numbers of African-American players.[2] The short-lived American Basketball Association, or ABA (1965–1977), functioned as another important showcase for paradigmatic black basketball talent such as the legendary Julius "Dr. J" Erving. Not only did the ABA's history parallel that of the Black Power Movement, but in crucial ways the ABA represented Black Power basketball.

"Dr. J's" high-flying, acrobatic dunk shots and innovative moves around the basket set new standards. His most famous dunk shot won the 1974 Slam Dunk Contest at the annual ABA All-Star Game. In a gravity-defying move, "Dr. J" leapt from the free-throw line, twelve feet from the basket, soared through the air, and, at the height of his midair trajectory, rammed the ball through the rim.[3] On another occasion, in one of his most re-played moves, he appears to be laying the ball in the basket on one side of the rim, only to duck under the rim to the other side, where he deftly lays the ball off the backboard into the basket, all the while evading his defensive man.

Given that the upstart ABA had more black players from its inception, the league featured the black basketball aesthetic to a greater degree than the NBA. The more flamboyant ABA show-cased a more black-inflected style of play: a more individualistic, fast-paced, high-leaping, fancy-dribbling, outrageous-dunking, playground-inspired style of play. Large Afro hairdos, high-five hand claps, slamming soul music, and growing numbers of black fans proliferated. When the NBA and the ABA merged in 1977, the NBA experienced a transformative African-American cultural infusion.

The African-American aesthetic in basketball exudes imagination, creativity, speed, and verticality, or leaping ability. Indeed, some of the most thrilling moments of the game, such as innovative dunk shots, take place above the ten-foot-high rim. The aesthetic also exudes signature styles in shooting, dribbling, and passing, topped off with supreme self-confidence. Freedom of movement and freedom of expression are basic to the open, fluid, and highly improvisational ethos of this aesthetic. Developed primarily on urban, often inner-city, playgrounds, it is an intensely masculine and extremely competitive domain where a black urban cool sensibility dominates.

No one better personifies this storied tradition and its ethos than seven-foot two-inch Harlemite Kareem Abdul-Jabbar (born Lew Alcindor). Particularly revealing of his quest for identity and meaning in the electric context of the late 1960s—especially Black

Power and Third World radicalism—were his controversial conversion to Islam and name change in the summer of 1968. Abdul-Jabbar's individual quest reflected the collective black emphasis on self-definition and self-affirmation so central to Black Power cultural politics. In this charged environment, innumerable blacks like Alcindor were drawn to Islam, especially its global humanism, or antiracism. In his own systematic search for "something to believe in," Alcindor had diligently pursued a comparative assessment of world religions. Particularly inspired by the shining example of Malcolm X, Alcindor soon found his way to the Sunni faith. Hamaas Abdul-Khaalis, Abdul-Jabbar's first Muslim teacher, named him Kareem ("noble," "generous") Abdul-("servant") Jabbar ("powerful"). "A man needs a new name," Abdul-Jabbar later noted. "Having recognized a different aspect of myself beginning to control the way I lived, I wanted and deserved a new identity."[4]

Throughout his college (UCLA, 1965–1969) and professional career (Milwaukee, 1969–1975; Los Angeles, 1976–1989), Abdul-Jabbar epitomized black urban cool on the basketball court: iconoclasm, unflappability, exceptional professional achievement, and thoroughgoing identification with the African-American community. His dominance at the collegiate level was so great that the rules committee disallowed the dunk shot. Their strategy failed, though. One consequence was that he developed a diverse array of moves close to the basket, most notably a beautiful and deadly accurate sky hook shot. To top it all off, he actively participated in the African-American Freedom Struggle and embodied the radical cultural politics of the Black Power era.

In homage to "jazz freedom fighter" John Coltrane, Abdul-Jabbar titled his 1983 autobiography *Giant Steps*, after one of Coltrane's tunes. The tribute uncannily captured a revealing resonance between Coltrane's and Abdul-Jabbar's cultural politics rooted in their common deep immersion in the wellsprings of African-American culture. A serious student of African-American history and culture, Abdul-Jabbar understood that his personal cultural politics built upon those of many unknown as well as acknowledged greats who laid the groundwork for his own development into a phenomenal player and for his equally extraordinary career.

That exceedingly rich groundwork included elements of the cultural politics of his immediate predecessors among great African-American basketball "big men," most notably Wilt Chamberlain and Bill Russell. Both were exceptional players, especially Chamberlain, and politically outspoken. The groundwork laid for Abdul-Jabbar also included the cultural politics of those like Coltrane, similarly deeply engaged in innovative and influential cultural work. Abdul-Jabbar's signature move came to be his elegant and unstoppable sky hook, a high-percentage shot that functioned as a powerful weapon in his diverse offensive arsenal. In a very real sense, Abdul-Jabbar built upon a powerful tradition of African-American genius seen across various cultural domains. Abdul-Jabbar played basketball like Coltrane played jazz: with improvisational flair, stunning virtuosity, and charismatic dignity.

In 1967, then collegian Lew Alcindor, already a cultural icon and a culture hero, joined a controversial black athletes' boycott of the 1968 Olympics. As one of the most accomplished, famous, and respected young athletes of his generation, his support for the boycott helped generate attention, negative and positive, for the action. That Alcindor was also widely respected as an intelligent and perceptive personality only enhanced his status as an exemplar of the movement. Like the leader of the boycott, Harry Edwards, a twenty-five-year-old assistant professor of sociology at San Jose State College and former athlete, Alcindor and his comrades condemned the pervasive antiblack racism of the American sports scene. Sports, they persuasively argued, reflected the deeply entrenched racism of the larger society. As a result, these protesting athletes committed themselves to mounting an offensive against racism in sports as part of the escalating antiracist insurgency so central to the Black Freedom Struggle, especially during the Black Power years.[5]

The defining moment of the boycott took place during the 1968 Mexico City Olympics. As part of the awards ceremony for the 200-meter dash,

> On 16 October 1968, Tommie Smith and John Carlos, two sprinters from San Jose State, mounted the awards platform to receive their gold and bronze medals. Both were shoeless and wore black, knee-length stockings and a black glove on one hand. Smith had a black scarf around his neck. When the band began to play the American national anthem, they sank chin to chest—seemingly to avoid looking at their country's flag. At the same time, their gloved fists shot skyward. Later, in an interview with Howard Cosell, Smith explained the symbolism of their actions. Their raised arms stood for the power and unity of black America. The black socks with no shoes symbolized the poverty that afflicted their black countrymen and women. Black pride was represented in Smith's scarf while the gesture of bowed heads was a remembrance of those like King and Malcolm X who had perished in the black liberation struggle.[6]

As William Van Deburg's taut description suggests, the deeply moving protest electrified countless numbers throughout the world. The radical black athlete, espousing a radical black cultural politics, had come of age. This stunning moment graphically captured the era's Black Power militancy. Almost immediately that powerful gesture achieved iconic status as a constantly recycled image, notably an immensely popular political poster. The black athletes who chose to boycott the 1968 Olympics vigorously supported the inspirational Smith-Carlos protest action.

Muhammad Ali personified this new breed of militant black male athlete. The 1960 Olympic heavyweight boxing champion before turning pro, then Cassius Marcellus Clay converted to the separatist Nation of Islam, or the Black Muslim faith, in the early 1960s under the leadership of the group's head, Elijah Muhammad, and tutelage of various ministers, including Malcolm X. Reflecting this conversion, Clay adopted the name Muhammad Ali. "Changing my name was one of the most important things that happened to me in my life," he explained. "It freed me from the identity given to my family by slavemasters . . . I was honored that Elijah Muhammad gave me a truly beautiful name. 'Muhammad' means one worthy of praise. 'Ali' was the name of a great general [a cousin of the prophet Muhammad]." Many at the time severely criticized his conversion. Declining to acknowledge his new name, some early on refused to use it, opting instead, like opponents Sonny Liston and Floyd Patterson, to call Ali "Cassius Clay." Hurt and angered, Ali demanded that he be called by his new name. Menawhile his commitment to Islam strngthened, in time becoming more orthodox.[7]

Unlike the cool and reserved public persona of Abdul-Jabbar, that of Muhammad Ali was brash and outspoken. Even before his stunning victory over the heavily favored Sonny Liston on February 25, 1964, when he first became world heavyweight champion, he was a master of prefight publicity and self-promotion. He rapped:

> I'm young, I'm handsome, I'm fast, I can't possibly be beat. I'm ready to go to war right now. If I see that bear [Liston] on the street, I'll beat him like I'm his daddy. He's too ugly to be the world champ. The world's champ should be pretty like me. If you want to lose your money, then bet on Sonny, because I'll never lose a fight. It's impossible. I never lost a fight in my life. I'm too fast. I'm the King.[8]

Self-professed and widely acknowledged as "the Greatest," Ali remade the American tradition of self-invention. Ali personifies that much-ballyhooed American freedom to make full use of one's talents, circumstances, and luck on the way to achieving greatness far beyond one's wildest dreams. As one of the most popular and widely admired personalities in the world since the 1960s, Ali reinvented and then expanded upon modern athletic stardom as a staging ground for unparalleled international celebrityhood. A critical aspect of this achievement has been Ali's identification with and call for a free, diverse, and tolerant America—and, by extension, a free, diverse, and tolerant world.

Ali's career inside and outside the boxing ring during the height of the Black Power insurgency had many high and low points. Throughout it all, his stock as a quintessential African-American, American, and international hero and celebrity soared. That he unfailingly and forcefully spoke his mind and willingly espoused controversial views, alternately thrilling and angering segments of the American population—indeed, the world—only enhanced his fame. His principled opposition to the Vietnam war along with his vigorous support for the Black Liberation Struggle marked him as a highly visible spokesman who embodied the militant black cultural politics of the era. Objecting to the Vietnam War on religious and moral grounds, Ali refused induction into the U.S. Army and engaged in a lengthy and costly legal battle to stay out of jail. Meanwhile he was forced to give up his passport. The boxing establishment also exacted punishment: Ali was stripped of his title and barred from fighting in the United States from 1967 to 1970, when he was at the peak of his physical powers. When he eventually regained the heavyweight boxing crown upon his return to the ring in the 1970s, Ali only magnified his public persona as "the Greatest."

So as not to unduly ruffle the white-supremacist status quo, most previous black heavyweight champions, with the notable exception of the rambunctious early twentieth-century champion Jack Johnson, were painfully restricted in what they could say and do. Ali, however, was different with a vengeance. Black, beautiful, and outspoken in the age of Black Power, Ali was also a tremendous boxer. He embodied the militant African-American "fury for liberty" and fired the popular imagination worldwide.

In his important 1968 collection of essays, *Soul on Ice,* Eldridge Cleaver insightfully characterized Ali as "the first 'free' black champion ever to confront white America." That freedom proved both essential and inspiring in the context of the times. An exemplar of black manhood as well as black peoplehood, Ali was, most significantly, his own person. In its emphasis on self-determination, Ali's own freedom struggle mirrored and pushed forward that of his people. Ali, Cleaver perceptively noted, was "determined not to be a white man's puppet even though he fights to entertain them; determined to be autonomous in his private life and a true king of his realm in public, and he is exactly that."[9]

In the 1960s Ali—whose boxing exploits redefined standards of virtuosity, improvisational flair, and achievement—emerged as an unrivaled symbol of the modern American experience itself. Not only did he personify his people's freedom struggle, especially the radical black cultural politics of the era; he also personified the very complexity of American freedom. In fascinating ways, as the most famous American of the last half-century, Ali has come to symbolize the very notions of American self-invention and supreme confidence.

Not surprisingly, then, in addition to his self-conscious identification as a global citizen, at the same time Ali envisions himself as intrinsically black and American. For him the world and the nation, the latter understood as both the African-American and American nations, enrich each other. His sense of nationalism, therefore, like the best of American nationalism and African-American nationalism, expands outward into an open-ended cosmopolitanism: a global citizenship.

Ali's Americanism is both probing and tough-minded. Before their first 1965 heavyweight championship fight, Floyd Patterson impugned Ali's commitment to America because of his antagonist's more radical politics. The affable and conservative Patterson claimed that he was going to win so as to return the title to America. Ali's response was clear and resolute. He excoriated Patterson for representing the forces of reaction—in essence, for being an "Uncle Tom." Ali offered a different and competing vision of America as he explained: "the title already is in America, just see who I pay taxes to. I'm American."[10]

Ali's America, though, is ultimately neither white nor black. Instead, it is diverse, tolerant, and changing. At the time, Ali symbolized the intensifying vigor of the Black Liberation Insurgency and its increasingly visible impact on America and the world. Ali's broader cultural import thus represented and built upon the movement's growing strength and influence, as Cleaver noted in a rapturous embrace of Ali's victory over Patterson:

> The victory of Muhammmed Ali over Floyd Patterson marks the victory of a New World over an Old World, of life and light over . . . the darkness of the grave. This is America recreating itself out of its own ruins. The pain is mighty for every American black or white, because the task is gigantic and by no means certain of fulfillment.[11]

The struggle of black athletes like baseball pioneer Jackie Robinson and tennis great Althea Gibson as well as Muhammad Ali to represent themselves and their people with dignity and pride is both instructive and inspiring. Their personal stories illuminate their people's collective story as well as the African-American Freedom Struggle. These narratives illuminate the individual and collective dimensions of the black social imagination and black cultural politics of their respective eras. With the rise of mass media coverage of sports, notably television coverage, the broader impact of the black social imagination and black cultural politics as revealed in the world of professional sports has only grown and deepened. In turn, the ability of African-American athletes to operate as agents of change has likewise grown and deepened.[12]

Throughout the late 1960s and early 1970s, significant battles over cultural representations of African-Americans and the related argument for a distinctive African-American culture intensified. In telling ways, the often neglected expressive domains of dance and visual arts highlight the dynamic "fury for liberty" at the core of both the postwar African-American liberation struggle and the interwoven terrain of African-American cultural politics. Both the black struggle and the attendant black cultural politics illuminate the interrelationship between American history, culture, and identity and African-American history, culture, and identity.

The centrality of African-American social, or popular, dance to the history of American social dance has been firmly established. Reflective of the larger African-American cultural matrix out of which it emerges, black social dance showcases six defining characteristics, according to Jacqui Malone. In fact the "rhythm, improvisation, control, angularity, asymmetry, and dynamism" so vital to African-American social dance defines African-American expressive culture generally, especially African-American visual arts.[13] The black basketball aesthetic discussed in the previous section is just one domain in which this cultural fact is manifest.

The interactive relationship between dance and song is another salient feature of African-American expressive culture. Dance and song are symbiotic. At bottom this dance-song dynamic reflects the antiphonal structure likewise fundamental to African-American expressive culture. "To dance the song" is a popular vernacular expression of this vital cultural process. "To dance the song" similarly refers to specific cultural practices that actively meld dance and song.[14] It thus speaks of the inseparable singing and shouting so crucial to ecstatic praise behavior, the reiterative dance movements of singers performing singly and collectively, the inspired dancing of an audience listening and singing along to a vocal, even an instrumental, performance.

The awareness and representation of modern vernacular African-American dance as vernacular American dance has only grown over time precisely because of the predominance of African-American social dance. From the early century's cakewalk, to the Charleston of the 1920s, the lindy hop of the 1930s, the 1950s stroll, the funky chicken of the late 1960s, and beyond, the impress of black vernacular dance styles and aesthetics on American social dance, and by extension American culture, has been determinative.[15]

In the more "highbrow" and white-dominated worlds of concert dance, especially in ballet, there has been an ongoing battle over African-American access and impact as well as representation. In large part this resistance to African-American aesthetics and styles has reflected the predominance in these domains of clashing European-American aesthetics, styles, and power, in addition to outright antiblack racism. Not surprisingly, therefore, in the concert dance world of the Civil Rights–Black Power years, the African-American search for selfhood and freedom of expression has revealed a quintessential cultural battle.

In both concert dance and visual arts, African Americans married the quest for artistic excellence to issues of identity: representing simultaneously African-American dance, visual art, and culture, on one hand, and American dance, visual art, and culture, on the other. Out of the diverse and fertile African-American artistic imagination, in the context of an escalating African-American Freedom Struggle, emerged innovative, vibrant, and deeply influential work by a range of cultural warriors.[16]

This explosive black social imagination of the era spawned two world-class and internationally renowned dance institutions: the Alvin Ailey American Dance Theatre (1958) and the Dance Theatre of Harlem (1969). The Ailey company and Dance Theater of Harlem (DTH) are largely the embodiment of their respective visionary founders: Alvin Ailey and Arthur Mitchell. Both men, fighting against the severe racism in the concert dance world, carved out enduring institutions showcasing black choreographers, black dancers, black aesthetics, and in turn black cultural politics. These institutions have also served as havens, offering artistic homes, creative outlets, and performance opportunities for African-American dancers, not to mention other dancers of color as well as white dancers. Both institutions also have provided vital outlets for advancing black perspectives, traditions, and practices throughout the concert dance world.

Particularly valuable has been the repertorial function of the Ailey and DTH companies. Both have provided for the preservation as well as the performance of the neglected work of pioneering and top-notch African-American choreographers and dancers like Katherine Dunham, Talley Beatty, and Donald McKayle.[17] As a result, as key institutions within the concert dance world, DTH and the Ailey have been central to the modern redefinition of African-American dance as American dance and, by extension, African-American culture as American culture. This transformation has occurred largely as a result of both institutions' view and use of African-American history, culture, and identity as the basis for a broad humanistic outlook and practice. Both institutions thus reflect a syncretic and expansive view of modern dance and classical ballet. That view is likewise reflective of a correlative view of American and world cultures as syncretic and expansive.

Blues Suite (1958) and *Revelations* (1960)—two of Ailey's most original and popular works—are steeped in the secular and sacred domains of African-American vernacular culture. These works brilliantly explore in symbolic and concrete ways specific African-American cultural practices associated with secular space—in effect, having a worldly good time—and sacred space—a religious good time. While working extensively with African-American cultural materials throughout his career, Ailey saw the dances themselves as universal in meaning, function, and appeal. For him, African-American culture was the springboard toward the universal. He was indeed a humanist, a cosmopolite, rather than a cultural or racial nationalist.

Early in his career, building upon the multicultural sensibility of Lester Horton, his mentor, Ailey had insisted that to conceive of dance in narrow racialist terms was misguided. "There is no such thing as Negro dance," he retorted to such representations of his work. In fact, he did not see himself primarily as "a black choreographer speaking to black people," but as an artist speaking to whoever would listen. Regarding *Revelations*, his most famous dance, he explained that it "comes from Negro spirituals and gospels. Its roots are in American Negro culture, which is part of the whole country's heritage. The dance speaks to everyone . . . Otherwise it wouldn't work."[18] In this view, African-American folk cultural materials, like those of any people, can and sometimes do function as the building blocks for world-class art with universal appeal.

Arthur Mitchell's guiding philosophy mirrors that of Ailey. Intensely proud of both his African-American heritage and his career as a topflight male ballet dancer for the New York City Ballet in the 1950s and 1960s, Mitchell brought impeccable credentials to his vision for an African-American classical ballet company. Through his company, Mitchell has remained committed to expanding African-American influence in the world of classical ballet. In addition, Mitchell sees his work as expanding the parameters of American culture as well as African-American culture. Nevertheless, classical ballet remains a very Eurocentric world, far more so than modern dance.

With its greater appreciation of indigenous and vernacular dance traditions, American modern dance has been far more open to African-American aesthetics, styles, and practices than American ballet. This fact has contributed to the warmer reception and greater success of the Ailey company, notably in the United

States. Modern American dance is far more comfortable with the energetic African-derived dance styles that help shape African-American dance. For instance, whereas classical ballet demands erect torsos and rigid pelvises, African and African-American dance demand shifting torsos and pelvises.

Modern dance is also more compatible with and sensitive to African-American bodies, especially fuller-figured African-American female bodies. The modern ideal of the classical balle-rina is waifishly thin, bordering on anorexic, with no curves, nota-bly tiny posteriors, and small breasts. Of course the physical re-quirements of classical ballet, especially dancing and spinning on one's toes and being lifted by male partners, impose certain weight and size limits for ballerinas. The physical appearance of ballerinas still reflects highly influential Eurocentric notions of female beauty: alabaster skin, sharp features, minimal lips, flow-ing straight hair pulled back in a tight bun. DTH has countered with a more Afrocentric female beauty aesthetic, notably a wider palette of skin hues. Still, the aesthetic is circumscribed in critical ways by tradition. In effect, while more sensitive to the range in African-American female bodies and notions of female beauty, the ostensible criteria for DTH ballerinas plainly reflect the need for smaller, less fully developed female bodies.

Mitchell's Dance Theatre of Harlem has done important work in making it possible for black women and men to become more fully accepted on their own terms in the conservative world of classical ballet. The company has generally prospered, but it has not approached the stratospheric success of the Ailey company. Nevertheless, Mitchell refuses to circumscribe his vision racially. He, like Ailey, sees his work as fundamentally an expression of both the Americanness of blackness and the universality of black-ness. Like the Ailey, the Dance Theatre of Harlem is a multiracial company and school. Mitchell is thus, like Ailey, a cosmopolite rather than a cultural nationalist or racial nationalist.

While the Ailey company works largely in the idiom of modern dance and DTH largely within that of classical ballet, both companies reflect a strong theatrical and commercial bent, especially the Ailey company. With the Dance Theatre of Harlem, Mitchell builds upon the classical ballet tradition, especially as reflected in the work of George Balanchine, his mentor, the twentieth century's greatest influence on American ballet. Mitchell's most innovative artistic contribution to the worlds of classical ballet in general and American ballet specifically has been the introduction of black themes, aesthetics, and styles. In *Creole Giselle,* Mitchell recreates and energizes the traditional ballet by staging it in Louisiana—as against courtly old Europe—and playing off of the racial, color, and class particularities of this vibrant New World setting.

Whereas Ailey founded his company in the early years of the modern Civil Rights Movement, Mitchell founded his at the height of the Black Power Movement amid the turmoil following the assassination of Martin Luther King Jr. on April 4, 1968. Indeed, Mitchell created his company out of a strong commitment to meld and advance the seemingly disparate interests of the besieged Harlem community and the ballet world. In creating his company at this pivotal moment of racial crisis, Mitchell vividly illustrated the relevance of black artistic excellence for ballet and, in turn, ballet's relevance for black artistic excellence. Mitchell's marriage of conservative ballet and assertive blackness thus transpires in the charged historical context of militant black cultural nationalism and increasing American cultural openness. The result has been striking and salutary.

Both Mitchell and Ailey, then, responded dramatically to the urgent need for world-class institutions in which black dancers could master their craft and perform at the highest level. Both also created schools to nurture future dance generations. In so doing, they contributed enormously to the complexity of the evolving black cultural politics of the 1960s and 1970s. Opting to create independent African-American institutions within the white-dominated concert dance mainstream, Mitchell and Ailey reflected a powerful and effective vision of black cultural politics at once evolutionary, pluralist, and integrationist.

The twentieth-century histories of the Dance Theatre of Harlem and the Alvin Ailey American Dance Theatre represent black cultural politics success stories. These histories similarly represent the realization of their founders' compelling visions. In this particular case, as elsewhere throughout this work, the concern with triumph and progress has obscured the difficulties and failures endured by innumerable African-American cultural warriors. Such experiences are most instructive. That discussion, though, is a separate one.

One lesson that emerges from the Ailey and DTH successes is the importance of long-term financial backing, be that funding stream white or black. It is clear that significant backing from white-identified sources has not diminished the Ailey's and DTH's commitment to African-American dance and African-American dancers. Nor has it diminished the stature of both institutions as emblematic of modern African-American concert dance.

The histories of both companies in this era illustrate the durability of the American success ideology and the resonance of that ideology for those engaged in the African-American Freedom Struggle. On a related level, both institutions vividly illustrate a multicultural and hybrid view of postwar America from the vantage point of black America. The operative black cultural politics in both of these cases is integrationist, inclusive, and expansive—indeed, in an important sense, global, yet rooted in blackness.

Historically, a broad range of representative African-American visual artists have also been concerned with issues of history, culture, and identity, notably since the second half of the nineteenth century. The art of the Harlem Renaissance and that of the related social realist period of the 1930s proved to be especially relevant to the later Civil Rights–Black Power era and the latter era's emphasis on a socially relevant art. The mid-1960s emergence of the Black Arts Movement and aggressive varieties of black cultural nationalism deeply influenced the era's visual art. The dramatic increase in the number and locations of African-American murals and political posters in the 1960s and 1970s, for instance, illustrates the didactic and polemical edge of the era's black cultural politics.[19] This openly political art, along with the rise in political artwork in other genres, like painting and printmaking, contrasts sharply with the more understated yet arresting work of artists like photographer Roy DeCarava.

The openly political art of the period—like the varying politics of the cultural work under consideration here—is essential to the powerful postwar rearticulation of both blackness and Americanness, separately and together. Work often seen as outside the purview of the black cultural politics of the era, like DeCarava's photographs and the religious art of Sister Gertrude Morgan, is linked intimately to it. These works illustrate a necessarily expansive view of the period's black cultural politics.

Between 1945 and 1975 there was a growing insistence among many artists that their work, while rooted in the African-American experience, must be understood as central to the redefinition of American art—and thus of American culture. Typically working outside the limited purview of the "official" American art tradition, with its Euro-American bias, these artists found inspiration in many places, notably Afrodiasporic ones. Particularly important in this regard has been the work of formally trained artists like Jacob Lawrence, Romare Bearden, and Elizabeth Catlett, all of whose careers bridge the earlier and later periods. Each of these artists in their own way saw their work reflecting and being influenced by the modern African-American Freedom Struggle. That influence and reflection deepened during the modern phase of the struggle. Catlett in particular directly inspired and engaged the period's militant cultural politics in her own work. Like their fellow cultural warriors, all these artists showcase various visions of blackness.

Lawrence's widely admired and influential Cubist-style paintings, notably of historical subjects, epitomize the way in which modern African-American art and African-American cultural politics have opened up the American art world and American culture conceptually and thematically, expanding notions of American art and culture. In particular, his *Toussaint L'Ouverture* series (1937–38), *Frederick Douglass* series (1938–39), *Harriet Tubman* series (1939–40), in concert with the most famous of all, *The Migration of the Negro* series (1940–41), demonstrate a level of uncommon achievement that his subsequent work did much to sustain and extend.[20]

One of Lawrence's paintings, *The Ordeal of Alice* (1963), is a probing assessment of the perils of integration, notably school integration (see Figure 1). The work vividly evokes the history of extraordinary black children warriors like the Little Rock Nine, who in 1957 valiantly pioneered southern school integration as the first black students to attend formerly all-white Central High in Arkansas' capital city. These young warriors bravely endured the fevered taunts of white crowds, extreme emotional and psychological assaults, the intense economic pressures on their families. Speaking to the assaults endured by those like Ruby Bridges, who single-handedly fought to integrate New Orleans elementary schools, the Alice of Lawrence's painting is a tragic, lonely figure.[21]

Christ-like in her suffering, Alice ultimately must bear the burden of school integration all alone. Surrounded and haunted by a series of ghoulish figures, Alice—starkly and minimally drawn—wears a white dress and white stockings pierced by arrows. So as to emphasize the brutality and trauma, the downcast black face sits angled on one edge of her neck. The costs of school integration for black children were exceedingly high; this work graphically suggests that it was too high.[22]

Like Ailey in modern dance, Lawrence excelled at the artistic representation of vernacular African-American experience in such a way as to highlight the Americanness—indeed the uni-

1. *Jacob Lawrence, The Ordeal of Alice, 1963.* © 2004 Gwendolyn
Knight Lawrence/Artists Rights Society (ARS), New York City.

versality—of that experience. That achievement has resonated
among audiences worldwide. The acclaim within the white-dominated art world that over time has greeted artists like Lawrence
has expanded the nation's cultural consciousness. At the height of
the polemics surrounding black art during the Black Arts Move-

ment, however, Lawrence's success within white establishment art circles led some militant artists to criticize him. They maintained that this achievement rendered Lawrence a sellout and distanced him from his people and their struggle.[23]

On the contrary, mainstream acclaim affirmed Lawrence's connection to his people and their struggle, and helped to enhance mainstream awareness of his people's struggles. The same point could be made regarding the emergence of Romare Bearden as a collagist extraordinaire in the 1960s, after his considerable earlier success as a painter in various styles. The best of these collages built upon his formidable eye and formal training, and constituted a pivotal shift from a more abstract phase to more strikingly representational yet highly stylized works. Here, as at other times during his career, there was a fertile tension between the abstract and the representational. These well-received and influential efforts explored in inventive and evocative ways various aspects of African-American culture: notably, music, ceremony, ritual; the rural South and the urban North; the mundane and the extraordinary. Bearden's collages resonated deeply with the spiraling "fury for liberty" of the postwar Black Liberation Insurgency.[24]

Inspired by legendary civil rights activist A. Philip Randolph's call for artists to bring to the Movement "a new visual order," Bearden joined with several of his African-American colleagues to create Spiral. This New York City–based group came together just before the Randolph-led 1963 March on Washington. Like many of their artist colleagues, they were concerned about the relationship between their people's freedom struggle in the South and their role as African-American artists. Out of that highly charged milieu emerged a major group show, "Black and White." Showcasing black-and-white prints and paintings in a variety of styles, the show reflected a gnawing but productive tension between the desire for color-blind recognition as visual artists and the desire to connect with their people's freedom insurgency. Illustrative of that tension, at Bearden's suggestion, Spiral changed the original title of the show from the openly political "Missis-sippi 1964" to the politically more ambiguous and evasive "Black and White.[25]

An unsuccessful effort among the Spiral group to create a collective mural led Bearden to use the material he had been col-lecting for the project to create what soon became his famous early photomontage series. The technique involved in part the photographic enlargement of small collages. The collages them-selves consisted of works built around paint, cut paper, and pho-tographs.[26] As evidenced in his profoundly affective piece *Conjur Woman* (1964), the multiple textures, inventive layering, striking juxtaposition of images, abstraction, and fractured lines and an-gles are shared by these works. These qualities give these works uncommon visual depth, insight, and intensity (see Figure 2). *Conjur Woman's* riveting eyes, for example, convey the sense of mystery and omniscience associated with conjure women.

Like *Conjur Woman,* as a body, the works in the series graphi-cally evoke mythic and ritualistic dimensions of African-Ameri-can history and culture. Drawing extensively upon his experiences in the rural black South of Mecklenburg County, North Carolina, and the urban black North of Pittsburgh and Harlem, Bearden created highly resonant folk, at times archetypal, images. His conjure woman, Gail Gelburd observes, is herself "the artist as al-chemist, seeking the philosopher's stone; the sorcerer telling of the myths of change and transformation; the soothsayer who will mark the future while recalling the past."[27] The strong, powerful women represented in *Conjur Woman* thus call to mind the tra-ditional community values and strong collective sensibility that characterized that community. These women personify the rich, accumulated wisdom of African-American folk knowledge.[28]

Bearden's later collage series *Of the Blues* (1975) showcases the musiclike qualities, notably the improvisational virtuosity, of his work. It likewise showcases his metaphoric use of music to repre-sent salient features of African-American history and culture.

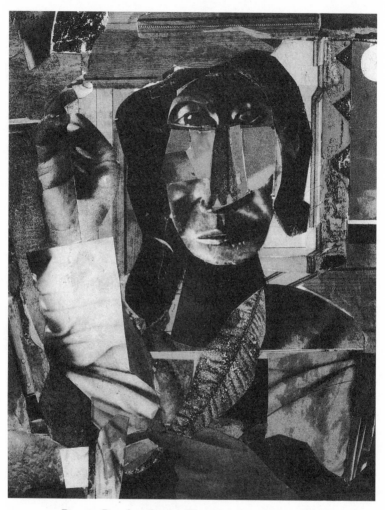

2. *Romare Bearden, Conjur Woman, 1964.* © Romare Howard
Bearden Foundation, Inc. / Licensed by VAGA, New York City.

Show Time (1975) centers on the classic African-American blues
woman, shades of Ma Rainey and Bessie Smith. To her right is a
super-cool trumpeter, reminiscent of jazz giant Miles Davis. To
her left is a trumpet player and vocalist, reminiscent of another
jazz giant, Louis Armstrong, with his signature handkerchief (see

Figure 3).[29] Not only are both the blues singer and the Armstrong figure engaged in a spirited duet, but both are also responding to the Miles-like character's riffs. The musicians are not only calling and responding to one another, but also calling and responding to the audience. The musical action epitomizes the antiphony characteristic of black music and culture.

Another interesting feature is the way in which the centered blueswoman bridges the older generation, personified by the Armstrong-like character, and the hip, new generation, personified by the Miles-like character. Here Bearden stresses the critical role of women as agents of social unity and continuity, as agents of cross-generational understanding as well as agents of cross-generational cultural transmission. Without this work, collective unity is impoverished and collective struggle is impossible. The blueswoman thus represents the centrality of black women's strong voices and their too often unheralded cultural work to a meaningful rendering of African-American experience generally, and African-American struggle more specifically.

A principal concern of this discussion thus far has been to illustrate the synergy between the Black Freedom Struggle, broadly conceived, and representative work of the two most renowned African-American visual artists of the period. A related concern has been to show an important continuity between African-American visual art traditions over the Depression-wartime era and the postwar freedom struggle era. In other words, the postwar African-American Freedom Struggle and the attendant African-American cultural politics reveal both salient shifts and equally salient carryovers from earlier periods. Most striking, though, is a fundamental continuity: the synergy between the freedom struggle and cultural politics, between art and politics.

The trajectories of the careers of Lawrence and Bearden illustrate this point. Personifying continuity of history, culture, and identity, Lawrence's striking Cubist-inspired collagist paintings since the late 1930s were consistently committed to a social realism influenced by the African-American experience. The twists

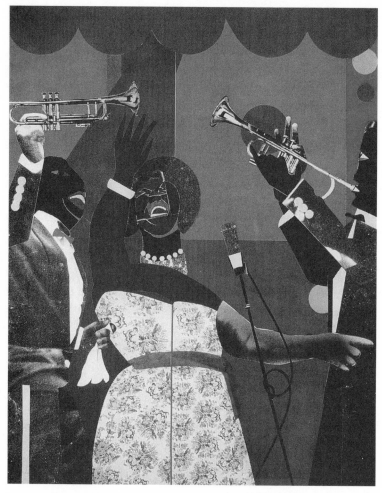

3. *Romare Bearden, Show Time, 1974.* © Romare Howard Bearden
Foundation, Inc. / Licensed by VAGA, New York City.

and turns of that experience greatly influenced his output but
did not substantially alter his trademark artistic vision and social
commitment. Lawrence's life and career thus reflected the tenac-
ity of his people's liberation struggle notwithstanding its inevitable ebb and flow.

Bearden's shift from the Abstract Expressionism of his 1950s work to his reinvention—and reinvigoration—of collage in the context of the rapidly escalating early 1960s Civil Rights Movement is most telling. The most revealing of these collages grow out of autobiographical memories. These works also showcase a far more conscious engagement with the whirlwind of the cultural politics of the overall movement. However, neither Lawrence nor Bearden produced political art in the didactic, narrow, and propagandistic sense of that term. Rather, both created rich and complex bodies of work with a far more nuanced edge that largely reflected its unwitting and witting resonance with their people's struggle.

A signal measure of their uncommon achievement is the fact that their artistic corpus, notably that of the 1960s, both engages and transcends the historical moment. It has stood the test of time. This is evident even in Bearden's early collages, notably the *Projections* series, with its probing dissection of memory, myth, and ritual. Myron Schwartzman has stressed the fact of "the lasting validity of the *Projections* . . . when many of the fashionable political and sociological styles of the 1960s now seem curios of a bygone era . . . Detached now from the rhetoric and emotion of the mid-1960s, which inevitably lent their reception an ambiance of political and social protest, the *Projections* seem more eloquent, the statement of a sensibility that was not caught up in the hurricane, but instead had found its eye."[30]

The same could just as easily have been said of the work of premier sculptor and printmaker Elizabeth Catlett. Yet while the American art establishment has welcomed the significant interventions of those like Lawrence and Bearden, it has been significantly less enthusiastic in its embrace of Catlett's equally original and powerful work. One reason is her status as a challenging and radical black woman artist, to the displeasure of many in the art establishment.

An undaunted cultural warrior, Catlett has been consistent in her vigorous support for an African-American art that directly and graphically engages the African-American Freedom Struggle. Catlett has been a driving force in the postwar effort to create innovative art that goes beyond social realism to social consciousness and political activism. Her cultural politics has much more in common than that of Lawrence and Bearden with the more aggressive black cultural politics of the 1960s, notably the radical black art of the Black Arts Movement. In its dogged insistence on blackness and feminism, not to mention Americanness, in crucial ways her work constitutes an even more challenging critique of the American art world and American culture than that of Bearden and Lawrence.[31]

Her numerous sculptures of the female form as well as mothers and children exude the warmth and virtuosity characteristic of her best work. A significant portion of that work treats women of color, especially black women, in stylized yet innovative ways. A key aspect of this body of work has been revisionist and reclamatory, even subversive, in the best sense. This work speaks persuasively to the importance of black women, in particular, representing themselves in affirmative ways. These strikingly affective artistic renderings of black women stress their dignity, strength, and beauty. As such, they constitute a powerful recasting of American as well as African-American history, culture, and identity.

Representations of African-American history, culture, and identity—not to mention American history, culture and identity—still far too often reflect an endemic sexism, racism, and classism. In contrast, the aesthetic central to Catlett's cultural politics stresses ordinary women and their experiences. Her work pushes forward the evolving progressive and multicultural understanding that gender as well as race and class must be factored into the ongoing reformulation of the American and African-American experiences, as well as global experience.

Catlett's radical politics and affiliations, along with her move to

Mexico in the 1950s, made her an object of Cold War and Red Scare repression, which contributed to her decision to become a naturalized citizen of Mexico in the early 1960s. This move did not lessen her commitment to the African-American Freedom Movement, however. In an important 1961 keynote speech before a meeting of art professors from southern black colleges, the National Conference of Negro Artists, Catlett issued a rallying cry, urging her fellow cultural workers to affiliate actively with their people's escalating freedom struggle personally, collectively, and artistically. On the question of whether or not black artists should define themselves in race-specific terms and act collectively, she was emphatic.

> Individual gains are limited by group advancement. A Negro artist is judged by the level of achievement of Negro artists as a whole, and the ones who excel will be included in American Artists to prove that in this branch of culture there is also democracy. We have to change our thinking on the question of group projects, group exhibitions, and united interests. After all, we are Negroes, and leaving out the word does not change the reality.[32]

Catlett saw this pluralist and activist commitment as essential to "the advance toward a richer fulfillment of life on a global basis. Neither the Negro artist nor American art can afford to take an isolated position."[33]

Catlett envisioned a black visual art aesthetic with an expanding range and influence. By looking more deeply to their people for inspiration and representing the essence of their people's history and culture, black visual artists, she believed, would be better able to create original and compelling art. The goal, she boldly asserted, was "to offer the world a Negro visual experience that will approximate the sincere and profound contribution of Negro music."[34]

The effect, reported Romare Bearden and Harry Henderson, was galvanic.

> Her words served as a powerful catalytic agent among black artists, asserting that their identity as African-Americans and their relationship to their people were critical in their development as artists and in gaining recognition. Her thoughts prompted black artists to organize groups to discuss their special problems as artists in America. While some of Catlett's ideas echoed those expressed by W. E. B. Du Bois in 1926, what gave them vigor and sharpness was the civil rights movement, the fierce concurrent struggle of colonial peoples in Africa and Asia to achieve independence, and the fact that black artists continued to be "overlooked" by those who controlled galleries and museums in the United States.[35]

Throughout the 1960s and 1970s Catlett created many sculptures and prints that directly addressed the concerns of the rising Black Power Insurgency. Catlett's *Homage to My Young Black Sisters* (1969) is a beautiful and affirmative representation of a young black woman in a vigorous, militant pose, her right fist raised directly to the sky in the stirring Black Power salute (see Figure 4). At the time, the Black Power salute was used in formal settings—such as political meetings—and informal settings—such as social situations—to signal solidarity with Black Power. *Homage to My Young Black Sisters* thus signified a firm commitment to the radical politics of the Black Liberation Insurgency and to the Black Power goals of black unity, self-definition, and self-determination.

Catlett's sculpture showcases her brilliant use of abstract, geometric forms to convey emotion and energy as well as to highlight the beauty of the human form. These aspects of Catlett's aesthetic sensibility have been heavily influenced by varieties of African sculpture.[36] *Homage to My Young Black Sisters* is a ringing endorse-

4. *Elizabeth Catlett, Homage to My Young Black Sisters, 1968.*
© Elizabeth Catlett / Licensed by VAGA, New York City.

ment of both young black women's radical political activism and the radical black politics of the time. The sleek, modernist female form symbolizes in part the tense relationship between women's liberation and black liberation, rejecting the racism of the former and the sexism of the latter. The singular intensity of the form attests to the need for a Black Freedom Struggle fully sensitive to the needs of black women. It strongly implies the need for a feminist struggle sensitive to the needs of black women, other women of color, and poor women.

The figure also speaks tellingly of the centrality of black women to the history of black activism and to Black Power activism in particular. The proud, forthright chin stands in for the absent head beyond the chin, and forces attention to the fist as symbolic of the head and mind, of spirit and consciousness. The torso opening is a testament of support for the expanding vistas for black women in the more progressive world envisioned by Black Power. "The opening in this figure's torso," as Melanie Anne Herzog has noted, "does not suggest emptiness but rather evokes the source of the energy carried upward in the raised fist." Furthermore, Herzog notes, "In a radical reclamation of women's role in the Black Liberation movement, this gesture . . . links the woman's procreative and revolutionary capacities."[37] The opening suggests that black women's procreative and political roles are both important and compatible. Seen another way, for black women committed to radical political activism, the political need not be subordinated to the procreative. Radical mothers, indeed mothers of the revolution, can and must be at once revolutionary and maternal.

Black Is Beautiful (1970) is representative of a body of prints from the era that illustrate Catlett's strong support for Black Power radicalism (see Figure 5). With a series of black women surrounding the face of Malcolm X, Catlett's *Malcolm X Speaks for Us* (1969) insists that the black nationalism personified by the fiery and influential leader X spoke to black women. The piece

5. *Elizabeth Catlett, Black Is Beautiful, 1970.*
© Elizabeth Catlett / Licensed by VAGA, New York City.

also insists that black nationalism had to be premised upon gender equality. With its incarcerated black male on the left, two armed white policemen without eyes (thus blind to justice) in the center, and four murdered black victims forming corners for the police figures, *Watts/Detroit/Washington/Newark* (1970) is a searing indictment of police brutality. This print vividly captures a deep-seated grievance within black communities that helped ignite a number of the black urban insurrections of the 1960s. *Homage to the Panthers* (1970) graphically portrays the leadership of the Black Panther Party and its insistence on the right of armed self-defense.[38]

In its serial display of the party's button featuring both the "Black Is Beautiful" slogan and the party's black panther, Catlett's *Black Is Beautiful* reiterates her vigorous support for the Black Panthers. In addition, the African masklike representation of the man and woman captures the moment's emphasis on black people being proud of their African-derived beauty, both its feminine and masculine forms, as well as their African cultural and historical connection.[39] The explicit linkage of the Panthers' militant political nationalism with their militant cultural nationalism exemplifies the cultural politics of Black Power. The importance of self-definition, self-determination, and self-esteem within this ethos is vividly rendered.

Inspired by the social consciousness of the 1930s Work Projects Administration art programs, Catlett's own art and cultural politics—like those of Lawrence and Bearden—valorized vernacular traditions as well as social consciousness. The concurrent radical politics and social consciousness of the Mexican painters and muralists deeply influenced all these, especially Catlett. An exemplar of the socially and politically committed artist, she has both passed on and enriched these important influences. Also, like the work of Lawrence and Bearden, Catlett's work points to important continuities in twentieth-century African-American visual art, notably the enduring concern with issues of self-identification and identity formation through art.[40]

There was a striking and influential body of African-American art in the Black Power years that reflected an intensely racialist, nationalist, even separatist aesthetic. Best seen as the visual wing of the Black Arts Movement, this work represented itself as a self-conscious, revolutionary break from integrationist/assimilationist cultural politics as well as a recovery and reconnection to nationalist/racialist/pan-African ties. The African Commune of Bad Relevant Artists (AFRI-COBRA) personified this increasingly popular vision. Begun in 1962 as an artists' workshop within Chicago's Organization of Black American Culture, this group evolved into one of the era's key exponents of a revolutionary art for the people. Their famous *Wall of Respect* (1967–1971) and *Wall of Truth* (1969) in Chicago's Southside epitomized the boom in African-American murals depicting heroes and history, and reflected the widespread effort to bring cultural nationalism to the masses.[41]

Unlike some nationalist organizations, AFRI-COBRA included women. AFRI-COBRA's emphasis on accessible and often pointedly antimodernist art, like so many such groups, also featured the production of poster prints, a popular contemporary medium. The cultural politics were militant, stressing black self-transformation as vital to Black Power Culture specifically, and to advancing the Black Freedom Struggle generally. This increasingly widespread view of black art at the time, according to Sharon F. Patton, featured "exhortations about unity, respect, and nationalism" that "use art as a pedagogical and ideological tool."[42] Yet like Bearden, Lawrence, and Catlett, the artists of AFRI-COBRA were concerned with the linkages among artistic aesthetics, racial identity, and politics or ideology.

Black art in this period was especially diverse, including artists who reveled in being seen as black artists and those who preferred to be seen primarily as artists. Nevertheless, increasing attention to the complexities of black history, culture, and identity earmarked this moment's visual art. Despite the efforts of artistic ideologues to fix notions of blackness, in the end the best work resisted such efforts. In fact, in its insistence on a multidimensional representation of black history, culture, and identity sensitive to the imperatives of diversity and differences in class, race, and gender, the work of Catlett showcases a crucial point of discontinuity with a narrower, notably masculinist, cultural politics of the past. Important and instructive in this regard in this period is the work of artists like painter and assemblagist Faith Ringgold.

A significant portion of Ringgold's compelling body of work explores issues of gender and sexuality as well as issues of race. A self-consciously feminist art, or women's art, much of her work exemplifies an important transition to an avowedly black feminist aesthetic in the black visual arts in the late 1960s and early 1970s. The centrality of the wide-opened mouths of her *Aunts Edith and Bessie* (1974), in the life-sized mixed-media installation series *Family of Women,* symbolizes "the need for women to speak out for themselves," writes Samella Lewis. Militant and black nationalist in emphasis, Ringgold's black female nude in her multipaneled *Slave Rape* series (1972) compellingly represents the history of the sexual abuse of black bodies—particularly black women's bodies.[43] In both works, the crying need for all, but especially women, to resist actively patriarchy as well as racism and classism is compellingly represented.

This kind of work typified the visual wing of a radical cultural politics associated with the wide-ranging Black Arts Movement. The key difference, building upon the pioneering work of those like Catlett, is the powerful gender critique. As the artistic front in the Black Power insurgency, such work represents in part a shift toward the reimagining of stereotypical Negroes, notably women, as defiantly black.

Betye Saar's seductive aesthetic sensibility reveals a vision of the artist as shaman. Key components of Saar's extensive body of work are her provocative 1970s and beyond found-art object assemblages and installations that evoke the deep spiritual power of objects. Through the manipulation and juxtaposition of found objects, including flea-market finds, as well as imagery culled from mundane and popular cultural sources, this work challenges us to think of alternative, even traditional, visions and belief systems. Third World and nonwestern sources as well as autobiographical and ancestral concerns contribute to this complex aesthetic vision. Her *Spirit Catcher* (1976–77) is a dense, pyramidlike pastiche that vividly illustrates the importance of alternative cultures and spiritualities to her aesthetic vision. In one section of the work, observes Peter Clothier, "Bones, shells, and feathers embellish the altar, along with religious symbols—the Star of David and the Islamic crescent, Egyptian ankh and rosary beads, reminding us that Saar's vision is inclusive and that it is the totality of the human spirit that she seeks to catch."[44]

While a significant portion of the art of Betye Saar thus resists racial and gender labels, a significant part of it offers a profound commentary on those very labels. In the late 1960s and early 1970s Saar created a powerful series of works within small boxes that graphically subverted various negative black stereotypes. This work speaks profoundly to issues of politics, race, and gender. But even these political works evoke the spiritual, the mystical. "They're all coffins," as Saar later described the boxes. "They contain relics from the past."[45] As symbols and visions, these relics offer intriguing narratives.

The Liberation of Aunt Jemima (1972) is a provocative critique in a mixed-media box of various versions of this archetypical image in the consumer universe (see Figure 6).[46] This work subverts the derogatory image of the dark, rotund, happy-go-lucky Negro maid as saleswoman through a self-transformation into a gun-toting revolutionary. The black clenched fist, symbolic of Black

6. *Betye Saar, The Liberation of Aunt Jemima, 1972.* Mixed media, 11 3/4 ´ 8 ´ 2 3/4 inches. University of California, Berkeley, Art Museum; purchased with the aid of funds from the National Endowment for the Arts (selected by the Committee for the Acquisition of Afro-American Art). Photo by Ben Blackwell. Courtesy of the artist.

Power militancy, enhances the tie to contemporary political stri-dency. This invigorating makeover slices against gender and racial stereotypes and represents an assertive black identity as gendered as well as racialized.

Ultimately, however, taken as a whole, Saar's work demands that we view identity—like its attendant history and culture—as multifaceted. In addition, the range and depth of her body of work speaks to the impulse among many black artists to envision themselves as artists in humanistic as against racialist terms. In its highly original way, then, Saar's work, like that of the other artists discussed thus far, illustrates a black cultural politics that opens outward onto the wider world, serving as a springboard for inclu-sive, expansive visions.

The foregoing visual artistic evidence reveals the influence of a growing pluralist sensibility in the United States sparked in sig-nificant ways by a black cultural politics tied to the African-American Freedom Struggle. An especially revealing piece of evi-dence of this development has been the increasing postwar popu-lar and critical valorization of the southern African-American folk artist. In part this growing appreciation of self-taught artists reflects the increasing appreciation of folk practices more gener-ally, such as folk music and storytelling. It also reflects the blur-ring between high and low culture. In addition, it reveals a cul-tural fascination with traditional, or roots, forms and expressions and what they tell us about cultural authenticity. Lastly, this fasci-nation speaks to the valorization of ordinary folk—the masses—common to the period's social movements, especially Civil Rights–Black Power.

The best of these self-taught artists are visionaries—often reli-giously inspired—who work out of a deep-seated inner drive. Their visions are often intensely personal and highly idiosyn-cratic. Operating outside the conventional art world, they and their work have come to represent a kind of artistic freedom and authenticity of expression untainted by ego and the market.[47] In

*7. Sister Gertrude Morgan, The Book of Revelation, ca. 1965–
1970.* Reproduced by permission of the owner, Dr. Siri von Reis.

many cases, spiritual and mystical muses shape the freedom that
these southern African-American self-taught artists exude. Sister
Gertrude Morgan's religiously inspired paintings showcase a fertile visual imagination seeking to spread the evangelical Christian
message. *The Book of Revelation* (ca. 1965–1970) is a six-foot, hori-
zontal window shade with angels, humans, animals, and snatches
of verse from the actual book of Revelation: a vivid representation
of heaven as paradise, the "New Jerusalem" (see Figure 7). This
powerful vision of earthly freedom as necessarily linked to heavenly freedom is a staple of Christianity, especially African-American varieties of Christianity.

In American Christianity, and especially in its African-American varieties, this expansive and multifaceted vision of freedom
has assumed influential forms that have sustained the ongoing
African-American Freedom Struggle. First, there is the important idea that Christians are God's chosen people. Their earthly
freedom, extending this position, is inevitable, as their liberty is
seen as part of God's design. Second, related to these notions of
Christian exceptionalism and God's active intervention in history

on behalf of his people, is the belief that this land, this United States, is a special place where African Americans are a crucial part of the unfolding of God's providential designs. This deeply influential Americanization of Christian exceptionalism has decisively shaped the larger secularized notion of national exceptionalism. As such, this American exceptionalism has assured Americans, in this case African Americans, that God is on their side.

One of the most interesting features of works like those of Sister Gertrude Morgan is its artful melding of the sacred and secular dimensions of exceptionalism. "The boldly colorful style, dense yet accessible iconography, and wonderful speaking power of an artist like Sister Gertrude Morgan," notes Susan Larsen, resonates deeply with the broader historical context. Morgan's work is that of an American visionary: a most revealing "part of a larger search among her generation for enduring spiritual values in an age of marked stress and doubt."[48] A parallel and related development is the centrality of religious/spiritual visions in black art more generally. As seen in the work of artists like Saar, Bearden, and Lawrence, this religious/spiritual nexus constituted another continuity between the earlier and modern Civil Rights generations. This nexus likewise united self-taught and trained black artists.

Black photographs have played a key role in presenting and representing the twentieth-century African-American experience. The two principal bodies of black photographic expression are the social and the documentary. Social photographs, the largest category, capture humanity in its variety, uniqueness, and commonality, showcasing posed and spontaneous moments, from the utterly ordinary to the extraordinary. These emphasize positive, uplifting images, what Nicholas Natanson calls the "visually upbeat."[49] This category would include amateurs and professionals committed to representing blacks in ways they themselves want to be seen.

Documentary photographs, typified by Depression-era "hard times" images of migrant workers and sharecroppers, reveal a more political aesthetic, an ideological point, an oppositional or critical vision. They resist "conventions and clichés." In turn, they evoke our empathy, invite our concern, and at times, as in the case of images of impoverished children in dire need, compel us to act. This sense of urgency, of wrestling honestly with harsh realities seen in the best documentary photographs, taps into an expansive sense of community.[50]

Particularly revealing in black photo historical representations has been the impact of the drama of the African-American Freedom Struggle. Indeed, that drama functions as an actual and subliminal context in which we see and understand these photographs, whether made by nonblacks or blacks. Here the distinctions between the social and the documentary blur as the photographic image enters the terrains of racial politics and black cultural politics. Especially when filtered through the lens of African-American history and culture, social photography can and does serve documentary functions. In part this dual role can be seen in the opposition of black social photography to stereotyped images of blacks and its call to expand our sense of community. Similarly, the best familial portraiture illuminates the universal through the specific. These family photographs tap deeply into the family drama, regardless of race.

Similarly, in part documentary photography can and does serve functions very much like those of social photography. This similarity can be seen best in the frank engagement in documentary photography with the social worlds of African Americans: at home, at church, at school, at work, and at play. It can likewise be seen in its struggling with how best to represent African Americans. What are the possibilities for not just getting beyond the stereotypes, but for honest and revealing portraits of ordinary black life?[51] Those possibilities are insightfully glimpsed in classic photographic work by Gordon Parks and Roy DeCarava.

The tradition of documentary photography, which the Farm Security Administration (FSA) photography unit under Roy Stryker thrust into the limelight, influenced DeCarava, but especially Parks. During his early 1940s stint working under Stryker, Parks honed his skills, interacting with an impressive group of documentary photographers, including Ben Shahn and Dorothea Lange. Angered by the oppressive Jim Crow restrictions in Washington, D.C., Parks set out to indict racism with his camera. This propagandistic impulse led to what is perhaps his most famous photograph, "Ella Watson" (1942). In that work, stoic charwoman Ella Watson poses with a mop in one hand and broom in the other, standing before a draped American flag in the background (see Figure 8). Through his effort to create that photograph, Parks learned a vital lesson. "I had learned how to fight the evil of poverty—along with the evil of racism—with a camera," he would often subsequently acknowledge.[52]

The photograph's very calculated composition parodies Grant Wood's famous painting *American Gothic* and its representation of the American Dream. Contrasted with that reassuring heartland painting featuring the white farmer with pitchfork in hand next to his white wife in front of their picturesque home, Parks's photograph is a biting black critique of the American racial nightmare. While Parks would later characterize the photograph as lacking in subtlety, it is precisely this lack of subtlety—the skilled use of the camera as a blunt weapon in the African-American Freedom Struggle—that makes the photograph so effective. It is the propagandistic edge of the photograph seen in its historical setting that gives the photograph its visual wallop. According to Parks, Ella Watson cleaned the office of a white woman with comparable credentials who had joined the government workforce at a lower-level job at the same time. That anonymous woman had been able to ascend to a desk job while Watson remained trapped in her subservient one.[53]

Parks's arresting series of photographs of Ella Watson presents

8. *Gordon Parks, "Mrs. Ella Watson, Government Charwoman," 1942.* Farm Security Administration, Library of Congress, Washington, D.C.

her with dignity and sensitivity, spotlighting one of the countless black victims of Jim Crow in the nation's capital. He allows Watson what Natanson calls "some spiritual and intellectual breathing room" in the photographs that capture her life outside her low-paying government job. This "breathing room" is especially apparent in the photographs of her home life and her experiences as a member of Saint Martin's Spiritual Church. One of the most interesting of these shows Watson with her three small grandchildren to the left, a mirror image of her adolescent adopted daughter to the right, and a framed photograph of an older couple in the middle. In this artfully composed photograph one can see the cross-generational hopes of early World War II black America: childhood dreams, adolescent longing, and mature retrospection. The hope and affirmation projected by the principals in the photograph contrast mightily with the shabby interior of the working-class home (see Figure 9).

Parks's popular and influential body of photographic work since the early 1940s has covered a vast array of topics. Still, even though the United States has come a long way since 1942, when these photographs were taken, they continue to resonate as a powerful critique of American racism, notably for African Americans and others trapped at the lower end of the socioeconomic system. In addition, they continue to speak evocatively, notably from the perspective of black working-class life, to the undeniable necessity of an ongoing African-American Freedom Struggle.

The work of DeCarava can perhaps best be categorized as modernist art photography. It exemplifies the power of the vernacular—especially images of ordinary folk, as well as the stuff of daily life artfully rendered—to capture the human spirit and human interiority. DeCarava is a master of chiaroscuro and of the naturally lit photograph, and his portraiture in particular captures African-Americans in subtle yet illuminating detail. In *The Sweet Flypaper of Life* (1955), DeCarava's compelling photographs of Sister Mary Bradley's Harlem family amplify Langston Hughes's

9. Gordon Parks, "Mrs. Ella Watson with Three Grandchildren and Adopted Daughter," 1942. Farm Security Administration, Library of Congress, Washington, D.C.

poignant text. These photographs capture the ability of Sister Mary Bradley's family, seen principally through her eyes, to find joy amid the trials of an admittedly difficult life.[54]

These images belong to a series of photographs of two Harlem families DeCarava shot in 1952 and 1953. The Bradley name is a fictionalized identity around which Hughes crafted his narrative. DeCarava shot the photographs as part of his year as the first African-American winner of the prestigious Guggenheim Fellowship for photography. His fellowship application had sketched out a grandiose proposal:

I want to photograph Harlem through the Negro people. Morning, noon, night, at work, going to work, coming home from work, at play, in the streets, talking, kidding, laughing, in the house, in the playgrounds, in the schools, bars, stores, libraries, beauty parlors, church, etc. . . . . I want to show the strength, the wisdom, the dignity of the Negro people. Not the famous and the well-known, but the unknown and the unnamed, thus revealing the roots from which spring the greatness of all human beings . . . I do not want a documentary of sociological statement. I want a creative expression, the kind of penetrating insight and understanding of Negroes which I believe only a Negro photographer can interpret. I want to heighten the awareness of my people and bring to our consciousness a greater knowledge of our heritage.[55]

This call for a "racially expressive art" at once socially relevant and universal was a lofty goal. Nevertheless, it was a goal that DeCarava, like Parks, managed to achieve.

Like Parks's classic portrayal of Ella Watson and her family, *The Sweet Flypaper of Life* is a critical meditation on an African-American working-class vision of the postwar American Dream. Taken in the early 1950s at the dawn of the modern African-American Civil Rights Movement, the photographs, like the text, project a sense of hope and affirmation, indeed aspiration, sorely tested in the earlier moment of Parks's photograph of Ella Watson. By the mid-1950s, the *Brown* decision and the Montgomery bus boycott had added fuel to the spreading Civil Rights Movement fire. As Sister Bradley explained, she was not ready to go home to meet her Lord, because she wanted to "stay here and see what this integration the Supreme Court has done decreed is going to be like."[56]

DeCarava's stunning "Mississippi Freedom Marcher" (1963) graced the promotional poster for the nationwide traveling exhibition of his work (1996–1999) (see Figure 10). Far more political

10. *Roy DeCarava, "Mississippi Freedom Marcher," 1963.*
Courtesy of the Smithsonian American Art Museum.
Museum purchase made possible by Henry L. Milmore.

than the photographs in *The Sweet Flypaper of Life*, it pointedly engages the prospects and perils of the American Dream. Taken at a critical moment in the Civil Rights Movement, this arresting photograph foregrounds an earnest and committed young African-American woman while shading a partial image of an African-American man in the right background. Without the caption, the photograph bears no telltale, clear-cut relationship to the 1963 March on Washington. The notables and protest signs are absent; the crowd is obscured. Instead, the young woman radiates a warmth, a passion, a sense of conviction that transcend that famous historical moment. Like so much of DeCarava's work, as Peter Galassi reminds us, "Mississippi Freedom Marcher" must be read as neither "a passive mirror" nor "an impassioned manifesto of the civil rights movement."[57]

DeCarava himself saw the photograph's subject in expansive humanist terms rather than narrow racial ones. He characterized the photograph as representing, in Galassi's words, "the beauty of human promise, not the struggle for racial equality."[58] In fact the photograph functions simultaneously, interactively, and inseparably as both humanistic and racialistic. The photograph works as both a social document and an artistic statement. It reflects a modernist sensibility at once aesthetically keen and politically engaged.

"Mississippi Freedom Marcher" also speaks to a commitment to group-based struggle. In 1963 DeCarava's concern for his people's plight and the racist discrimination black photographers endured as a group led him to join the Kamoinge Workshop. This impressive, loose-knit group of photographers adopted for their name the Kikuyu word for collective effort. Over the years the group has met to exchange ideas and to critique members' work. Like the Spiral group led by Romare Bearden, the photographers of the Kamoinge Workshop married political awareness to a probing modernist aesthetic. Throughout the years, Kamoinge's aim has remained "to seek out the truth inherent in our cultural roots: to create and communicate these truths with insight and integrity." Even though DeCarava formally left the group in 1965, his influence has persisted.[59]

As in his poignant photographs for *The Sweet Flypaper of Life,* in the riveting "Mississippi Freedom Marcher" DeCarava captures a historical moment pregnant with possibility, a defining American moment. Throughout much of his varied and fascinating body of work, there is what Sherry Turner DeCarava describes as an "understated quiet tonality" that is particularly evident in "the poetry of his landscapes."[60] It is the synergy between that most seductive tonality and the equally, if not more, seductive compositional improvisation that proves so arresting. This synergistic effect is particularly pronounced in his classic photography of jazz musicians in performance. His "Coltrane on Soprano" (1963) captures the jazz giant at a moment of deep musical concentration and churning emotional intensity, typifying DeCarava's masterful painterly eye.[61]

Like Parks's photographs of Ella Watson and her family, DeCarava's "Mississippi Freedom Marcher" is a representative American photograph. Such photographs "are not simple depictions but constructions," according to Alan Trachtenberg. Consequently, "the history they show is inseparable from the history they enact." The photographs of Parks and DeCarava are essential to a larger historical and cultural project: "a history of photographers employing their medium to make sense of their society." The best photographic work in this light, as James Guimond notes, crafts "an idea of what America should (or should not) be into the visual fact of a photographic image in as truthful a way as possible."[62] This highly interpretive gesture—this quest for a larger pattern of cultural connection and historical meaning—is central to postwar black cultural politics and the correlative freedom struggle.

The photographic work of Parks and DeCarava thus demonstrates how professional issues become wittingly and unwittingly intertwined with the cultural politics of the Black Freedom Struggle. Their work is clearly a vital part of what Trachtenberg has characterized as the very important "history of photographers seeking to define themselves, to create a role for photography as an American art."[63] Like painters, sculptors, and other kinds of visual artists, photographers like DeCarava and Parks built upon visual artistic conventions like composition and portraiture not just to represent reality, but to see it through fresh and original eyes. The work of Parks and DeCarava, however, is much more than a mere aspect of the history of the professional and artistic coming-of-age of photography as an artistic genre. Like the diverse work of the other African-American cultural warriors discussed here, their work is about a far more probing and revealing historical consideration. That is: Why, how, and with what consequences has African-American culture shaped American culture, and, by extension, global culture? This expansive body of work demonstrates that to "Be Real Black for Me," as Roberta Flack and Donny Hathaway asked in their 1972 song, is no easy task.[64]

Black to the Future

YOUTH ACTIVISM WAS a central feature of the 2002 antiwar movement. Widespread opposition to the U.S. war in Iraq was especially intense and pervasive in the San Francisco Bay Area. One reason was the area's unusually vigorous left-progressive tradition of antiwar activism, with strong support from an unusually high number of activist youth organizations and movements. From the official rallies to the local youth-led marches and teach-ins, the message was resoundingly clear and pointed. Similarly, in various influential youth media outlets—including pamphlets, newsletters, newspapers, and local youth television and radio programming—the message was disseminated widely and persuasively by many hip-hop journalists but also through events organized by the Berkeley La Peña Cultural Center's "Collective Soul," the Oakland Mandela Arts Center's "Freestyle Friday," and "raptivist" organizations such as Underground Railroad and Youth Force Coalition. These Bay Area youth framed the war in Iraq as an arrogant imperial adventure manifesting a half-baked and unjustifiable U.S. policy of aggressive unilateralism.

The key expressive framework for the oppositional movement

was hip-hop culture. In the militant messages and rocking cadences of youth antiwar rhetoric, in strident rap music new and old, in hard-hitting spoken-word poetry, on eye-catching graffiti-inspired billboards and murals, at antiwar concerts and impromptu antiwar gatherings, the substantive and stylistic imprint of hip-hop culture was ubiquitous and profound. Especially noteworthy was the youth programming on the Berkeley-based, left-progressive Pacifica radio station KPFA, where on Hard Knock Radio, led by longtime hip-hop activist and community leader David "Davey D" Cook, every weekday afternoon youth articulated an antiwar message from a variety of telling angles. These included the war's ominous meanings for the disproportionate number and percentage of youth of color who would inevitably fight and die in the conflict. Much concern was likewise expressed about the potentially devastating economic, political, social, and cultural consequences of the war for future generations.

In the late 1990s I dropped in on a memorable jazz concert headed by the outstanding Brooklyn-based saxophonist Steve Coleman and a strong group featuring local musicians. The playing, especially by Coleman, was energetic. What really captured my attention that evening, however, was the warm-up act: the Invisibl Skratch Picklz, an all-star disk-jockey band featuring "DJ Qbert," "D-Styles," and "Shortkut." Manipulating their turntable systems, these DJs made the trademark scratching sound by manipulating both records back and forth in movements both spontaneous and polished. Throughout, the emphasis on improvising upon the beat, inside and outside of it, created a music at once edgy and incantatory, new and old: a compelling hybrid music. They reworked and played upon the beats taken from the breaks of different songs where, in the words of the inimitable James Brown, the musicians "give the drummer some." Using these beats, they launched a polyrhythmic attack, deepened by various electronic manipulations. Pumping out booming instrumental and vocal sounds, punctuated by staccato, at times booming vocal accents, they shook the rafters of that club. They cut, mixed, scratched, and improvised off of beats and riffs from a stunning array of musical sources, notably classic James Brown and jazz grooves. The musical amalgam was never less than fascinating, and often mesmerizing. Little did I know at the time that they just happened to be among the most widely revered and influential DJs in the world.

That performance by the Invisibl Skratch Picklz struck me in a number of ways both at the time and in retrospect. Particularly riveting was the elemental power of the call-and-response structure within the music created by each DJ, among the three DJs, and between the DJs and the audience. Like the music's improvisational richness, its hypnotic rhythmic drive, and its insistent dance grooves, the structure confirmed the blackness of the sonic and participatory experience. Equally striking was that in dress, movement, and word, that is, visually and stylistically, as well as musically, the performance epitomized a hip-hop aesthetic and ethos.

Similarly noteworthy was the fact that while they stunningly performed a set of musical practices rooted in blackness, the DJ crew was Filipino American. Blackness, like hip-hop, has clearly come to be understood as inclusive and open rather than exclusive and closed. In today's postmodern, post–Civil Rights, post–Black Power world, blackness, like hip-hop, has come increasingly to be seen as residing not in an embodied essence, not in any outmoded and discredited biophysical notion of "race."

Instead, this view of blackness, again like hip-hop, is increasingly seen as signifying an evolving transracial culture, an evolving transracial consciousness and way of life. Popular, and therefore still influential, notions of blackness and of hip-hop as synonymous with a fixed, unchanging notion of race are inaccurate and misleading. Its nationalistic, separatist, and exclusivist varieties notwithstanding, hip-hop, like blackness, must be additionally understood, and I argue ultimately better understood, as moving toward the humanistic and universalistic.

Today my undergraduate students at Berkeley, regardless of their racial identifications, typically see hip-hop culture as a defining element of their generation. They almost universally applaud hip-hop's widespread appeal and the voice it provides for the marginalized and the oppressed. At the same time, these students criticize what they see as endemic problems owing to hip-hop's inextricable ties to the larger culture. These encompass the larger culture's co-optive and mollifying capitalist dynamic: its ability to defang hip-hop's oppositional qualities and to make major money off of it, all at the same time.

Many rail against the crass commercialization and commodification of hip-hop, against a capitalist marketplace shot through with structural inequities based on racism and sexism. They perceptively critique a system and its ignominious history in which those who create and innovate, notably black creators and innovators, too seldom reap the profits from their work. While they bemoan the ongoing exploitation and theft of black creativity for the enrichment of others, they nonetheless applaud the fact that more and more blacks are now beginning to reap some of the profits from hip-hop.

Proposals for a fairer, more equitable system vacillate between a redistributionist capitalism and a strong democratic socialism. In the end, for all its apparent oppositional and transformative potential, hip-hop tends to mimic many of the worst features of the society of which it is a part, and in doing so reinforces them. Those students most concerned with a more effective oppositional hip-hop culture persuasively tend to connect that culture to more vigorously anticapitalist positions.

Almost all these students are taken with the beats and the music at the core of hip-hop culture. Almost all are deeply aware of the blackness at the root of that culture. Many, regardless of race/

ethnicity, embrace that blackness, in particular its more universalistic and humanistic expressions. Many do not know what to make of it. Many shy away from it. Fortunately, a growing number seek to understand it. A common refrain heard well beyond Berkeley—notably among white middle-class urban/suburbanites—is that hip-hop culture, especially the best of rap music, is devoted to "keeping it real." "In spite of the artifice, imitation, and philosophical quicksand so intrinsic to what we popularly characterize as real," notes Miles Orvell, "popular notions of an essential, irreducible reality persist."[1] The notion of "realness" as rooted in hip-hop culture signifies an authenticity of experience and profundity of understanding that most of us desire. In contrast, many, notably innumerable white suburban youth, see their own world as boring, stultifying, even alienating.

The notion of the authenticity of experience and profundity of understanding rooted in hip-hop, and by extension in blackness, reflects the fascination with blackness and hip-hop as sites of pleasure, especially forbidden, exotic, even primitive visions of pleasure. In part, this notion also reflects a guilt born of enjoying race-based and class-based privileges perceived as rooted in a fundamentally unjust system. In part, it calls forth another belief: the notion of suffering and oppression as not only morally ennobling, but also as a basis for a deeper, richer, and thus more revelatory life experience. Among the oppressed this view tends to enhance both self-esteem and a sense of efficacy. This cluster of beliefs suggests that surviving, especially transcending, oppression in crucial ways has made the oppressed stronger and more resilient than the oppressor. In the art world, this kind of understanding is consistent with the view that great artistic achievement is the result of tortured genius.

A critical look at the recent history of both hip-hop and blackness thus illuminates the parallel and related history of black cultural politics. In the twenty-first century, black popular culture has come to dominate American popular culture. Hip-hop culture in particular powerfully shapes and represents international and domestic dimensions of American popular culture. Everywhere you look, from products to advertising and marketing, the global culture that is preeminently American culture is often black, hip-hop, or inflected in those directions. Reflective of this dominance is the fact that for the first time in its history, the Billboard Music Chart for mid-October 2003 listed ten songs by black artists as the ten top-selling songs. All were artists working within the hip-hop domain.

Because mass-mediated varieties of American popular culture are the key engine driving popular world cultural expressions, the global impact of hip-hop culture is huge. Homegrown varieties of rap music, often giving voice to the concerns of outsiders and dissident youth, can be heard from Cuba to Japan. In the Bronx, notably the Bronx River Parkway Apartment Complex, the graffiti art, break dancing, DJs, emcees, and b-boy and b-girl styles that coalesced as hip-hop culture emerged as a cluster of street cultural practices in the mid-1970s. The subsequent global mushrooming of hip-hop culture demonstrates the vitality and universality of black expressive culture and the continuing importance of black cultural politics.

Hip-hop's emergence at the moment of transition from the era of Black Power to a post–Black Power era is part of an increasingly expansive black consciousness attuned to its global dimensions, both within and beyond the African diaspora. The expansion of this black consciousness was manifest in the intensifying American campaign against South Africa's apartheid regime and the ongoing assault against comparable forms of American apartheid. Indeed, the voice of hip-hop vigorously reflected and pushed forward the antiapartheid struggle at home and abroad.

Hip-hop signifies a postmodern elaboration on the recurrent historical theme of a black cultural politics at once black and humanistic. Hip-hop exudes a postmodern sensibility, questioning simplistic modern verities such as unalloyed linear progress and challenging both the enduring reality of white supremacy and the falseness of the American Dream. This postmodern sensibility can also be glimpsed in hip-hop's highly inventive aesthetic emphasis on collage, or pastiche, and creolism, or hybridity most visible in the borrowed and mixed bases of the graffiti art and the layered and quiltlike quality of the music.

The vision of a singular and coherent race-based Black Freedom Struggle largely prevailed throughout the 1960s. Despite the internal fissures within that movement, especially during the Black Power years, the center held. In the last quarter of the twentieth century, however, the center fractured, particularly around issues of political strategies/tactics, class, gender, leadership, and intergenerational conflict. No longer is there a geographic center of the Black Freedom Struggle as, say, the South was in the Civil Rights era, and the North and West were at the height of Black Power. No longer can a single person be said to speak for all of black America. And today the ways in which black cultural politics mirror and contribute to that struggle are no less complex.

After the 1970s the Black Freedom Struggle became a far more decentered and complicated series of local, regional, national and international struggles. The hip-hop generation took root and flowered in this context. They have come of age with the recent history of Civil Rights and Black Power movements as contested memory, if not simply forgotten or ignored. Nevertheless those historic struggles function more and more as bases upon which the politically aware hip-hop generation constructs its own present-day struggles and identifications.

The post–Black Power era has witnessed the continuing economic stagnation and decline of inner-city black communities, and the devastating consequences of this seemingly inexorable trend. Class-based rifts among blacks are accelerating, notably between the middle class who have fled those communities and the underclass and working class who are unable to leave. Hip-hop culture, especially rap music like that of KRS-One and Black Star, focuses on these vital concerns. Economic empowerment was a key aspect of the Civil Rights and Black Power movements. Hip-hop culture's continuing engagement with the issue reveals its growing centrality not only to the contemporary Black Freedom Struggle but also to the interrelated black cultural politics.

In a February 1968 speech delivered in California, Ethiopian emperor Haile Selassie starkly posed a critical challenge confronting black cultural politics, Africans throughout the diaspora, indeed people everywhere. He resolutely predicted that until the global scourge of white supremacy was fully abolished everywhere, there would be no peace. In a powerful song built around that speech, reggae giant and hip-hop icon Bob Marley affirmed the reverberating warning that the inevitable consequence of maintaining this intolerable situation would be widespread "War."[2]

Notes

Introduction

1. Michael Denning, *The Cultural Front: The Laboring of American Culture in the Twentieth Century* (London, 1996); Lawrence Levine, *The Opening of the American Mind: Canons, Culture, and History* (Boston, 1996); Charles M. Payne, *I've Got the Light of Freedom: The Organizing Tradition and the Mississippi Freedom Struggle* (Berkeley, 1995); Robin D. G. Kelley, *Race Rebels: Culture, Politics, and the Working Class* (New York, 1994); William Van Deburg, *New Day in Babylon: The Black Power Movement and American Culture, 1965–1975* (Chicago, 1992). For British cultural studies, see David Morley and Kuan-Hsing Chen, eds., *Stuart Hall: Critical Dialogues in Cultural Studies* (London, 1996); Kobena Mercer, *Welcome to the Jungle: New Positions in Black Cultural Studies* (London, 1994); Paul Gilroy, *The Black Atlantic: Modernity and Double Consciousness* (Cambridge, 1993); Hazel Carby, *Cultures in Babylon: Black Britain and African America* (London, 1999); Houston A. Baker Jr., Manthia Diawara, and Ruth Lindeborg, eds., *Black British Cultural Studies: A Reader* (Chicago, 1996).

2. Arjun Appadurai, *Modernity at Large: Cultural Dimensions of Globalization* (Minneapolis, 1996), 14.

3. Mercer, *Welcome to the Jungle*, 16; Ross Posnock, *Color and Culture: Black Writers and the Making of the Modern Intellectual* (Cambridge, Mass., 1998), 9.

4. Ralph Ellison, *Shadow and Act* (New York, 1964).

5. Steven Lawson, *Running for Freedom: Civil Rights and Black Politics in America since 1941*, 2d ed. (New York, 1997); Robert Weisbrot, *Freedom Bound: A History of the Civil Rights Movement in America* (New York, 1990); Harvard Sitkoff, *The Struggle for Black Equality, 1954–1992*, rev. ed. (New York, 1993); Manning Marable, *Race, Reform, and Rebellion: The Second Reconstruction in America, 1945–1990* (Jackson, Miss., 1991); and Benjamin Muse, *The American Negro Revolution* (Bloomington, 1968).

6. Michael Denning has written that cultural politics refers to "the infrastructure of any cultural initiative, the necessary world of publishers, galleries, salons, patrons, and reviewers by which artists and audiences are recruited and mobilized, and without which no cultural formation can take root"; *The Cultural Front*, 202. For a perceptive recent study of black cultural politics during this period, see Suzanne E. Smith, *Dancing in the Street: Motown and the Cultural Politics of Detroit* (Cambridge, Mass., 1999). Like that of Denning, her work builds upon the concept of cultural

formation popularized by Raymond Williams in two essays: "The Future of Cultural Studies" and "The Uses of Cultural Theory." See Raymond Williams, *The Politics of Modernism* (London, 1996); Scot Brown, *Fighting for US: Maulana Karenga, the US Organization, and Black Cultural Nationalism* (New York, 2003).

7. Larry Neal, *Visions of a Liberated Future: Black Arts Movement Writings*, ed. Michael Schwartz (New York, 1989), x, xi.

8. Vincent Harding, *Hope and History: Why We Must Share the Story of the Movement* (Maryknoll, N.Y., 1990), 127, 141; Edward Said, *Culture and Imperialism* (New York, 1993), 212.

9. For a good discussion of the notion of a cultural front, see Denning, *The Cultural Front.*

10. Appadurai, *Modernity at Large,* 7.

11. "Review Essays: What's Beyond the Cultural Turn?" *American Historical Review* 107 (December 2002), 1475–1520.

12. Robin D. G. Kelley, *Yo' Mama's Disfunktional! Fighting the Culture Wars in America* (Boston, 1997), 124.

1. "I, Too, Sing America"

1. Lance Jeffers, "My Blackness Is the Beauty of This Land," in *Black Fire: An Anthology of Afro-American Writing,* ed. LeRoi Jones and Larry Neal (New York, 1968), 273–274.

2. Patrick Rael, *Black Identity and Black Protest in the Antebellum North* (Chapel Hill, 2001); Adam Fairclough, *To Redeem the Soul of America* (Athens, Ga., 1987); Leonard I. Sweet, *Black Images of America, 1784–1870* (New York, 1976).

3. Jeffers, "My Blackness Is the Beauty of This Land."

4. Dominic J. Capeci Jr. and Martha Wilkerson, *Layered Violence: The Detroit Rioters of 1943* (Jackson, Miss., 1991).

5. John Hope Franklin and Alfred A. Moss Jr., *From Slavery to Freedom: A History of African-Americans,* 7th ed. (New York, 1994), 445.

6. Henry Louis Gates Jr., *Colored People: A Memoir* (New York, 1994), 85.

7. Waldo E. Martin Jr., *Brown v. Board of Education: A Brief History with Documents* (Boston, 1998), 1–41.

8. Robert L. Carter, *A Matter of Law: A Memoir of Struggle in the Cause of Equal Rights* (New York, forthcoming); John Dittmer, *Local People: The Struggle for Civil Rights in Mississippi* (Urbana, 1994), 1–40; Timothy B. Tyson, *Radio Free Dixie: Robert F. Williams and the Roots of Black Power* (Chapel Hill, 1999), 27–89.

9. I am indebted to Marge Frantz for the formulation of "The Great Repression."

10. Stephen J. Whitfield Jr., *A Death in the Delta* (Baltimore, 1988).

11. Fannie Lou Hamer's speech is well presented in the classic documentary *Eyes on the Prize: America's Civil Rights Years, 1954 to 1965, Part One, Episode 5: Mississippi—Is This America?* (Alexandria, Va., 1993). See also Chana Kai Lee, *For Freedom's Sake: The Life of Fannie Lou Hamer* (Bloomington, 1999); Kay Mills, *This Little Light of Mine: The Life of Fannie Lou Hamer* (New York, 1993).

12. David J. Garrow, *Bearing the Cross: Martin Luther King, Jr., and the Southern Christian Leadership Conference* (New York, 1986), 283–86, speech quoted on 284.

13. "This Is My Country," in *The Best Impressions* (Buddah, 1970).

14. Marvin E. Jackmon, "Burn, Baby, Burn," in Jones and Neal, *Black Fire,* 269; Gil Scott-Heron, *The Revolution Will Not Be Televised* (Flying Dutchman, 1974).

15. Penny M. Von Eschen, *Race against Empire: Black Americans and Anticolonialism, 1937–1957* (Ithaca, 1997).

16. James H. Meriwether, *Proudly We Can Be Africans: African-Americans and Africa, 1935–1961* (Chapel Hill, 2002).

17. Frantz Fanon, *The Wretched of the Earth* (New York, 1967); Ronald Takaki, *Double Victory: A Multicultural History of America in World War II* (Boston, 2000); Michael Omi and Howard Winant, *Racial Formation in the United States: From the 1960s to the 1990s,* 2d ed. (New York, 1994); Robert Blauner, *Still the Big News: Racial Oppression in America* (Philadelphia, 2001).

18. Countee Cullen, "Heritage," in *The Norton Anthology of African-American Literature,* ed. Henry Louis Gates Jr. and Nellie Y. McKay (New York, 1997), 1311.

19. Meriwether, *Proudly We Can Be Africans.*

20. Jennifer Hochschild, *Facing Up to the American Dream: Race, Class, and the Soul of the Nation* (Princeton, 1995), xii.

21. Lawrence W. Levine, "The Concept of the New Negro and the Realities of Black Culture," in *The Unpredictable Past: Explorations in American Cultural History* (New York, 1993), 106.

22. Stokely Carmichael and Charles V. Hamilton, *Black Power: The Politics of Liberation in America* (New York, 1967), 55.

23. Ibid., 47. See also William Van Deburg, *New Day in Babylon: The Black Power Movement and American Culture, 1965–1975* (Chicago, 1992), 113–129; Harold Cruse, *The Crisis of the Negro Intellectual: From Its Origins to the Present* (New York, 1967).

24. Elizabeth Hutton Turner, "The Education of Jacob Lawrence," in *Over the Line: The Art and Life of Jacob Lawrence,* ed. Peter T. Nesbett and Michelle DuBois (Seattle, 2000), 100.

25. Michael Denning, *The Cultural Front: The Laboring of American Culture in the Twentieth Century* (London, 1996), xviii.

26. Robin D. G. Kelley, *Hammer and Hoe: Alabama Communists during the Great Depression* (Chapel Hill, 1990), 92–116, 107.

27. Gunnar Myrdal, *An American Dilemma: The Negro Problem and Modern Democracy* (New York, 1944), 928.

28. John Blassingame, *The Slave Community: Plantation Life in the Antebellum South,* rev. ed. (New York, 1979); Lawrence W. Levine, *Black Culture and Black Consciousness: Afro-American Folk Thought from Slavery to Freedom* (New York, 1977); Sterling Stuckey, *Slave Culture: Nationalist Theory and the Foundations of Black America* (New York, 1987); Robin D. G. Kelley, *"Yo' Mama's Disfunktional! Fighting the Culture Wars in Urban America* (Boston, 1997).

29. Maxine A. Craig, *Ain't I a Beauty Queen? Black Women, Beauty, and the Politics of Race* (New York, 2002); Van Deburg, *New Day in Babylon.*

30. Cruse, *Crisis of the Negro Intellectual;* Harold Cruse, *Rebellion or Revolution* (New York, 1968).

31. Catherine Macklin, "Global Garifuna: Negotiating Belizean Garifuna Identity at Home and Abroad," in *10th Annual SPEAR Studies on Belize* (Belize City, 1994), 6–7.

32. Craig, *Ain't I a Beauty Queen?*

33. Sociological discussions of social movements are a good starting point for a consideration of these kinds of issues. See Enrique Larana, Hank Johnston, and Joseph Gusfield, eds., *New Social Movements: From Ideology to Identity* (Philadelphia, 1994); Hank Johnston and Bert Klandermans, eds., *Social Movements and Culture* (Minneapolis, 1995).

34. Reginald Jones, *Black Psychology,* 2d ed. (New York, 1980); Levine, *Black Culture and Black Consciousness;* Stuckey, *Slave Culture.*

35. Clarence Walker, *Deromanticizing Black History: Critical Essays and Reappraisals* (Knoxville, 1991).

36. Sweet, *Black Images of America,* 147.

37. Stuckey, *Slave Culture,* ix, 98–137, 303–358.

38. Levine, *Black Culture and Black Consciousness,* 444–445.

39. Berry Gordy, *To Be Loved* (New York, 1994); Nelson George, *Where Did Our Love Go* (New York, 1986); Suzanne E. Smith, *Dancing in the Street: Motown and the Cultural Politics of Detroit* (Cambridge, Mass., 1999).

40. John A. Kouwenhoven, *The Beer Can by the Highway: Essays on What's "American" about America* (New York, 1961), 53.

41. Robert G. O'Meally, ed., *The Jazz Cadence of American Culture* (New York, 1998), xi.

42. Kouwenhoven, *The Beer Can by the Highway,* 72.

43. Nathan I. Huggins, "Afro-American History: Myths, Heroes, Reality," in *Key Issues in the Afro-American Experience,* ed. Nathan I. Huggins, Martin Kilson, and Daniel M. Fox, vol. 1 (New York, 1971), 17.

44. Giles Gunn, *The Culture of Criticism and the Criticism of Culture* (New York, 1987), 150.

45. Langston Hughes, *Selected Poems of Langston Hughes* (1959; reprint, New York, 1990), 275.

2. *"Spirit in the Dark"*

1. *Aretha Franklin, Queen of Soul: The Atlantic Recordings* (Rhino, 1992).

2. Nikki Giovanni, "Poem for Aretha," in *The Women and the Men* (New York, 1975).

3. Bruce Smith, "Voice of Aretha in Italy," in *Mercy Seat* (Chicago, 1994), 36.

4. E. Ethelbert Miller, "The Voice of Aretha Franklin Surprised Me," *Carolina Quarterly* 50 (Fall 1997), 62.

5. Robert Shelton, "Songs a Weapon in Rights Battle: Vital New Ballads Buoy Negro Spirits across the South," *New York Times*, August 15, 1962, 1, 14. The passage refers to President John F. Kennedy and local Albany chief of police Laurie Pritchett. For more on the Freedom Songs, consult *Freedom in the Air: The Civil Rights Movement in Song*, three audio-tape set (Media Works, 1997); *Voices of the Civil Rights Movement: Black American Freedom Songs* (Smithsonian Institution, 1980).

6. Shelton, "Songs a Weapon," 1, 14.

7. Ibid.; Chana Kai Lee, *For Freedom's Sake: The Life of Fannie Lou Hamer* (Bloomington, 1999); Kay Mills, *This Little Light of Mine: The Life of Fannie Lou Hamer* (New York, 1993).

8. Howard Zinn, *SNCC: The New Abolitionists* (Boston, 1964), 4; Sterling Stuckey, "Going through the Storm: The Great Singing Movements of the Sixties," in *Going through the Storm: The Influence of African American Art in History* (New York, 1994), 267.

9. Robin D. G. Kelley, *Freedom Dreams: The Black Radical Imagination* (Boston, 2002), 11–12.

10. Mary C. Waters, *Ethnic Options: Choosing Identities in America* (Berkeley, 1990), 147–168.

11. Michael Omi and Howard Winant, *Racial Formation in the United States: From the 1960s to the 1990s* (New York, 1994); William J. Wilson, *The Declining Significance of Race: Blacks and Changing American Institutions* (Chicago, 1980).

12. Stephen Henderson, *Understanding the New Black Poetry: Black Speech and Black Music as Poetic References* (New York, 1973), 18; Robert B. Stepto, "Teaching Afro-American Literature: Survey or Tradition: The Reconstruction of Instruction," in *Afro-American Literature: The Reconstruction of Instruction*, ed. Robert Stepto and Dexter Fisher (New York, 1979), 18. For an interesting criticism of Stepto see Houston Baker Jr., "Discovering

America: Generational Shifts, Afro-American Literary Criticism, and the Study of Expressive Culture," in *Blues, Ideology, and Afro-American Literature: A Vernacular Theory* (Chicago, 1984), 90–97; Norman Harris, *Connecting Times: The Sixties in Afro-American Fiction* (Jackson, Miss., 1988), 6–7.

13. Claude McKay, "If We Must Die" (1919), in *The Norton Anthology of African-American Literature*, ed. Henry Louis Gates Jr. and Nellie Y. McKay (New York, 1997), 984.

14. *The Marcus Garvey Papers*, ed. Robert Hill, 9 vols. (Berkeley, 1983–1995); Lawrence Levine, "Marcus Garvey and the Politics of Revitalization," in *Black Leaders of the Twentieth Century*, ed. John Hope Franklin and August Meier (Urbana, 1982), 105–138.

15. Margaret Walker, "For My People" (1942), in Gates and McKay, *Norton Anthology of African-American Literature*, 1572–73.

16. Ibid., 1573.

17. Larry Neal, *Visions of a Liberated Future: Black Art Movement Writings* (New York, 1989). See also *Callaloo* 8:1 (1985), an issue dedicated to Neal's work.

18. Haki R. Madhubuti, Introduction to *Think Black!* (1966), in *Groundwork: New and Selected Poems from 1966–1996* (Chicago, 1996), 5.

19. Mari Evans, "Speak Truth to the People," in Henderson, *Understanding the New Black Poetry*, 253.

20. John Litweiler, *The Freedom Principle: Jazz after 1958* (New York, 1984), 13–14.

21. Cornel West, *Race Matters* (New York, 1994), 105.

22. Scott DeVeaux, *The Birth of Bebop: A Social and Musical History* (Berkeley, 1997); David H. Rosenthal, *Hard Bop: Jazz and Black Music, 1955–1965* (New York, 1992); John F. Szwed, *Space Is the Place: The Life and Times of Sun Ra* (New York, 1997), 232.

23. Len Lyons, *The 101 Best Jazz Albums: A History of Jazz on Record* (New York, 1980), 164; Thelonius Monk quoted in ibid., 165; Ortiz M. Walton, *Music: Black, White, and Blue* (New York, 1972), 104; W. T. Lhamon Jr., *Deliberate Speed: The Origins of a Cultural Style in the American 1950s* (Washington, D.C., 1990).

24. Rosenthal, *Hard Bop*, 43–45.

25. Charles Mingus, *Passions of a Man: The Complete Atlantic Recordings, 1956–1961* (1997); Le Roi Jones, *Blues People: Negro Music in White America* (New York, 1963); Rosenthal, *Hard Bop*.

26. Brian Ward, *Just My Soul Responding: Rhythm and Blues, Black Consciousness, and Race Relations* (Berkeley, 1998); Nelson George, *The Death of Rhythm and Blues* (New York, 1988); Craig Werner, *A Change Is Gonna Come: Music, Race, and the Soul of America* (New York, 1998).

27. Eric Porter, *What Is This Thing Called Jazz: African-American Musicians as Artists, Critics, and Activists* (Berkeley, 2001).

28. Nat Hentoff, liner notes to Max Roach, *Freedom Now Suite* (Columbia Contemporary Masters Series, 1960; reprint, 1980).

29. Litweiler, *The Freedom Principle*, 34.

30. I am indebted to Lawrence Levine for clarifying this point about similar developments in classical music and jazz.

31. Lyons, *The 101 Best Jazz Albums*, 373–374.

32. Litweiler, *The Freedom Principle*, 13.

33. John Coltrane, *The Complete Prestige Recordings* (1956–1958; remastered and rereleased, 1991); see also *Coltrane, The Classic Quartet—Complete Impulse! Studio Recordings* (GRP Records, 1998); Eric Nisenson, *Ascension: John Coltrane and His Quest* (New York, 1993); John Fraim, *Spirit Catcher: The Life and Art of John Coltrane* (West Liberty, Ohio, 1996); J. C. Thomas, *Chasin' the Trane: The Music and Mystique of John Coltrane* (New York, 1975); C. O. Simpkins, *Coltrane: A Musical Biography* (New York, 1976); Bill Cole, *John Coltrane* (New York, 1976); Frank Kofsky, *Black Nationalism and the Revolution in Music* (New York, 1970); Jack Boulware, "Requiem for a Church Supreme," *San Francisco Weekly*, January 28–February 1, 2000, 13–29; Francis Davis, "Coltrane at 75: The Man and the Myths," *New York Times*, September 23, 2001, Arts and Entertainment Section, 31.

34. Boulware, "Requiem for a Church Supreme."

35. For Coltrane's recording of "Alabama," see *The Smithsonian Collection of Classic Jazz*, record 12 (Smithsonian Institution, 1973); Coltrane quoted in Martin Williams' accompanying booklet, also titled *The Smithsonian Collection of Classic Jazz* (Washington, D.C., 1976), 43.

36. Lyons, *The 101 Best Jazz Albums*, 281; Kofsky, *Black Nationalism and the Revolution in Music*.

37. Ben Ratliff, "The Miracle of Coltrane: Dead at 40, Still Vital at 75," *New York Times*, December 7, 2001, sec. E1, 8; Michael S. Harper, *Dear John, Dear Coltrane* (Pittsburgh, 1970), 74–75.

38. Ward, *Just My Soul Responding*; George, *The Death of Rhythm and Blues*; Michael Haralambos, *Soul Music: The Birth of a Sound in Black America* (New York, 1974); Phyl Garland, *The Sound of Soul* (Chicago, 1969); Peter Guralnick, *Sweet Soul Music: Rhythm and Blues and the Southern Dream of Freedom* (New York, 1986), 7, 18.

39. *Aretha Franklin, Queen of Soul: The Atlantic Recordings*; Mark Bego, *Aretha Franklin: Queen of Soul* (New York, 1989).

40. Giovanni, "Poem for Aretha," 12–15.

41. Guralnick, *Sweet Soul Music*; William Van Deburg, *New Day in Babylon: The Black Power Movement and American Culture, 1965–1975* (Chicago, 1992).

42. Nina Simone, "Four Women," in *Wild Is the Wind* (Phillips, 1966); "Mississippi Goddamn!" in *Nina Simone in Concert* (Phillips, 1965); *Curtis Mayfield and the Impressions: The Anthology, 1961–1977* (MCA Records,

1992); Nikki Giovanni, "Revolutionary Music," in *Black Feeling, Black Talk, Black Judgment* (New York, 1970), 75–76.

43. West, *Race Matters*, 105; Askia Muhammad Toure quoted in Kelley, *Freedom Dreams*, 11–12.

44. LeRoi Jones quoted in Mel Watkins, "The Lyrics of James Brown: Ain't It Funky Now, or Money Won't Change Your Licking Stick," in *Amistad 2: Writings on Black History and Culture*, ed. John A. Williams and Charles F. Harris (New York, 1971), 22.

45. David Levering Lewis and Thulani Davis are quoted in Guralnick, *Sweet Soul Music*, 240, 242–243; Watkins, "The Lyrics of James Brown," 22; Imamu Amiri Baraka, *Funk Lore: New Poems, 1984–1995*, ed. Paul Vangelish (Los Angeles, 1996), 72.

46. Watkins, "The Lyrics of James Brown," 22.

47. James Brown, *Star Time* (Polydor, 1991).

48. George, *The Death of Rhythm and Blues*, 99; James Brown with Bruce Tucker, *James Brown: The Godfather of Soul* (New York, 1986), 228–233.

49. Rickey Vincent, *Funk: The Music, the People, and the Rhythm of The One* (New York, 1996); *Sly and the Family Stone: Greatest Hits* (Columbia, 1970); Sly and the Family Stone, *There's a Riot Going On* (Epic, 1971); Funkadelic, *Free Your Mind and Your Ass Will Follow* (Westbound Records, 1971).

50. Vincent, *Funk*, 19.

51. David Henderson, *Jimi Hendrix: Voodoo Child of the Aquarian Age* (Garden City, N.Y., 1978).

52. Porter, *What Is This Thing Called Jazz*.

53. A first-rate discography of Sun Ra's music compiled by Robert L. Campbell can be found in Szwed, *Space Is the Place*, 427–448.

54. Vincent, *Funk*, 138; Lyons, *The 101 Best Jazz Albums*, 400–402; Szwed, *Space Is the Place*. For an interesting set of 1960s poems by Sun Ra, see LeRoi Jones and Larry Neal, eds., *Black Fire: An Anthology of Afro-American Writing* (New York, 1968), 212–220.

55. Szwed, *Space Is the Place*; Leon F. Litwack, *"Been in the Storm So Long": The Aftermath of Slavery* (New York, 1978); Eric Foner, *Nothing but Freedom: Emancipation and Its Legacy* (Baton Rouge, 1976); Nina Simone, *Silk and Soul* (RCA, 1967).

56. Tony Heilbut, *The Gospel Sound: Good News and Bad Times* (New York, 1971); Michael Harris, *The Rise of Gospel Blues: The Music of Thomas Andrew Dorsey in the Urban Church* (New York, 1992).

57. Heilbut, *The Gospel Sound*; Harris, *The Rise of Gospel Blues*; Paul Oliver, "Gospel," in Paul Oliver, Max Harrison, and William Bolcom, *The New Groove: Gospel, Blues, and Jazz with Spirituals and Ragtime* (New York, 1980), 189–222.

58. Heilbut, *The Gospel Sound*, 31, 11.

59. Ibid., 10.

60. See the booklet by Bernice Johnson Reagon accompanying the three-album Smithsonian set *Voices of the Civil Rights Movement: Black American Freedom Songs, 1960–1966* (Smithsonian Institution, 1980), 4, 10, 17; Samuel Floyd, *The Power of Black Music: Interpreting Its History from Africa to the United States* (New York, 1995); Aretha Franklin, *Young, Gifted, and Black* (Atlantic, 1972).

61. Heilbut, *The Gospel Sound*, 13, 322.

62. Ibid., 13; Mahalia Jackson, *Gospels, Spirituals, and Hymns*, 2-CD set (Columbia, 1991); The Caravans, Featuring Shirley Caesar, *"Amazing Grace"* (Charly, 1991).

3. *"Be Real Black for Me"*

1. Booker T. Washington, *Up from Slavery*, ed. William Andrews (1901; reprint, New York, 1996), 15.

2. Nelson George, *Elevating the Game: Black Men and Basketball* (New York, 1992).

3. Ibid., 179–188.

4. Kareem Abdul-Jabbar and Peter Knobler, *Giant Steps* (New York, 1983), 165, 169.

5. Ibid., 170–172; Harry Edwards, *The Revolt of the Black Athlete* (New York, 1969).

6. William Van Deburg, *New Day in Babylon: The Black Power Movement and American Culture, 1965–1975* (Chicago, 1992), 90.

7. Muhammad Ali with Richard Durham, *The Greatest: My Own Story* (New York, 1975); Thomas Hauser, *Muhammad Ali: His Life and Times* (New York, 1991), 102.

8. Hauser, *Muhammad Ali*, 8.

9. Eldridge Cleaver, *Soul on Ice* (1968; reprint, New York, 1992), 92, 95.

10. Hauser, *Muhammad Ali*, 139–140.

11. Cleaver, *Soul on Ice*, 94.

12. On athletes as agents of social change, see Kathleen S. Yep, "They Got Game: The Racial and Gender Politics of Basketball in San Francisco's Chinatown, 1932–1949" (Ph.D. diss., University of California at Berkeley, 2002), 19.

13. Jacqui Malone, *Steppin' on the Blues: The Visible Rhythms of African-American Dance* (Urbana, 1996), 32.

14. Ibid., 28.

15. Ibid., 23–36; Katrina Hazzard-Gordon, *Jookin': A History of Social Dance Formations in African-American Culture* (Philadelphia, 1992).

16. Lynne Fauley Emery, *Black Dance from 1619 to Today* (1972; reprint, Princeton, 1988); Richard A. Long, *The Black Tradition in American Dance* (New York, 1989); Hazzard-Gordon, *Jookin'*; Malone, *Steppin' on the Blues*.

17. Thomas F. DeFrantz, *Dancing Revelations: Alvin Ailey's Embodiment of*

African American Culture (New York, 2004); Jennifer Dunning, *Alvin Ailey: A Life in Dance* (Reading, Mass., 1996); Alvin Ailey with A. Peter Bailey, *Revelations: The Autobiography of Alvin Ailey* (New York, 1995); Emery, *Black Dance*, 272–284; Long, *Black Tradition in American Dance*, 143–158.

18. Ailey quoted in Dunning, *Alvin Ailey*, 186, 243.

19. James Prigoff and Robin Dunitz, *Walls of Heritage, Walls of Pride: African-American Murals* (San Francisco, 2000).

20. Romare Bearden and Harry Henderson, *A History of African-American Artists from 1792 to the Present* (New York, 1993); Richard J. Powell, *Black Art and Culture in the Twentieth Century* (New York, 1997); Samella Lewis, *Art: African-American* (New York, 1978); Ellen Harkins Wheat, *Jacob Lawrence: American Painter* (Seattle, 1986); Peter T. Nesbett and Michelle DuBois, *Jacob Lawrence: Paintings, Drawings, and Murals (1935–1999): A Catalogue Raisonné* (Seattle, 2000); Myron Schwartzman, *Romare Bearden: His Life and Art* (New York, 1990); Ruth Fine, *The Art of Romare Bearden* (New York, 2003); Samella Lewis, *The Art of Elizabeth Catlett* (Claremont, Calif., 1984).

21. On the story of the Little Rock Nine, see Melba Patillo Beals, *Warriors Don't Cry* (New York, 1994); Daisy Bates, *The Long Shadow of Little Rock: A Memoir* (Little Rock, 1962). On Ruby Bridges, see Adam Fairclough, *Race and Democracy: The Civil Rights Struggle in Louisiana, 1915–1995* (Baton Rouge, 1995), 248–249.

22. Wheat, *Jacob Lawrence*, 108–110, 134.

23. Ibid., 191.

24. Schwartzman, *Romare Bearden*, 204–239, 209–211, 216–217.

25. Gail Gelburd, "Romare Bearden in Black and White: The Photomontage Projections 1964," in Gail Gelburd and Thomas Golden, *Romare Bearden in Black and White: Photomontage Projections 1964* (New York, 1997), 18–20, A. Philip Randolph quoted on 18; Sharon F. Patton, *African-American Art* (New York, 1998), 185–186.

26. Gelburd, "Romare Bearden in Black and White," 19–20.

27. Ibid., 36.

28. Romare Bearden, "Rectangular Structure in My Montage Paintings," *Leonardo* 2 (January 1969), 17, quoted in Gelburd and Golden, *Romare Bearden in Black and White*, 33.

29. Schwartzman, *Romare Bearden*, 230, 230–233, 275–278.

30. Ibid., 216.

31. Lewis, *Art of Elizabeth Catlett*; Bearden and Henderson, *History of African-American Artists*, 418–426.

32. Speech quoted in Lewis, *Art of Elizabeth Catlett*, 100.

33. Ibid., 98.

34. Ibid., 99.

35. Bearden and Henderson, *History of African-American Artists,* 424.

36. Melanie Anne Herzog, *Elizabeth Catlett: An American Artist in Mexico* (Seattle, 2000), 142–143, quotation on 142.

37. Herzog, *Elizabeth Catlett.*

38. Ibid., 136–142.

39. Ibid., 138.

40. Bearden and Henderson, *History of African-American Artists,* 418–426.

41. Powell, *Black Art and Culture,* 144–145; Patton, *African-American Art,* 214–215.

42. Patton, *African-American Art,* 215.

43. Lewis, *Art: African-American,* 146; Powell, *Black Art and Culture,* 148.

44. Peter Clothier, "The Other Side of the Past," in *Betye Saar,* exhibition catalogue, Los Angeles Museum of Contemporary Art (Los Angeles, 1984), 29, 35.

45. Ibid., 25.

46. Lewis, *Art: African-American,* 173, 171–174; Lowery Stokes Sims, "Artists, Folk and Trained: An African-American Perspective," in *Passionate Visions of the American South: Self-Taught Artists from 1940 to the Present,* ed. Alice Rae Yelen (Jackson, Miss., 1993), 35.

47. Alice Rae Yelen, "Self-Taught Artists: Who They Are," in Yelen, *Passionate Visions,* 18.

48. Susan Larsen, "A View of Paradise from a Distant Shore," in Yelen, *Passionate Visions,* 39.

49. Nicholas Natanson, *The Black Image in the New Deal: The Politics of FSA Photography* (Knoxville, 1992), 31.

50. James Guimond, *American Photography and the American Dream* (Chapel Hill, 1991), 9, 17.

51. Natanson, *Black Image in New Deal,* 46.

52. Carl Fleishhauer and Beverly W. Brannan, eds., *Documenting America, 1935–1943* (Berkeley, 1988), 226–239, photo on 235, Gordon Parks quoted on 229. See also "A Conversation with Gordon Parks," in Martin H. Bush, *The Photographs of Gordon Parks* (Wichita, 1983), 5, 38.

53. Fleishhauer and Brannan, *Documenting America,* 226–229.

54. Roy DeCarava and Langston Hughes, *The Sweet Flypaper of Life* (1955; reprint, Washington, D.C., 1984).

55. Peter Galassi, *Roy DeCarava: A Retrospective* (New York, 1996), 19.

56. Ibid.; James Alinder, ed., *Roy DeCarava: Photographs* (Carmel, Calif., 1981); DeCarava and Hughes, *The Sweet Flypaper of Life,* 9. I saw the exhibit "Roy DeCarava: A Retrospective" while it was at the San Francisco Museum of Modern Art, January 22–April 14, 1998.

57. Galassi, *Roy DeCarava,* 31.

58. Ibid.

59. Ibid., 32; Commentary, *Nueva Luz: Photographic Journal* 7:1 (2001), 33.

60. Sherry Turner DeCarava, "Celebration," in Alinder, *DeCarava: Photographs*, 14.

61. Ibid., plate 54.

62. Alan Trachtenberg, *Reading American Photographs: Images as History—Mathew Brady to Walker Evans* (New York, 1989), xvi; Guimond, *American Photography and the American Dream*, 18.

63. Trachtenberg, *Reading American Photographs*, xvi.

64. *Roberta Flack & Donny Hathaway* (Atlantic, 1972).

Epilogue

1. Miles Orvell, *The Real Thing: Imitation and Authenticity in American Culture, 1880–1940* (Chapel Hill, 1989), xvi.

2. Emperor Haile Selassie's speech quoted in Gladstone Wilson, "Reggae as a Medium of Political Communication," in *Mass Media and the Caribbean*, ed. Stuart H. Surlin and Walter C. Soderlund (New York, 1990), 439; Bob Marley and the Wailers, *Rastaman Vibration* (Island Records, 1976).

Credits

"No Coward Soldier," words and music by James Herndon. Copyright © 1963 (renewed) Conrad Music, a division of ARC Music Corp. (BMI). All rights reserved. Used by permission. International copyright secured.

"My Blackness Is the Beauty of This Land," from Lance Jeffers, *My Blackness Is the Beauty of This Land* (Detroit: Broadside Press, 1970). Copyright 1970 by Lance Jeffers. Reprinted by permission of Broadside Press.

"This Is My Country," words and music by Curtis Mayfield. Copyright 1968 by Warner-Tamerlane Publishing Corp. All rights reserved. Used by permission.

"The Revolution Will Not Be Televised," from Gil Scott-Heron, *So Far, So Good* (Chicago: Third World Press, 1990). Copyright 2003 by Gil Scott-Heron. Reprinted by permission of Third Word Press, Inc.

"Poem for Aretha," from *The Collected Poetry of Nikki Giovanni, 1968–1998* (New York: William Morrow, 2004). Copyright 2004 by Nikki Giovanni. Reprinted by permission of the author.

"Voice of Aretha in Italy," from Bruce Smith, *Mercy Seat* (Chicago: University of Chicago Press, 1994). Reprinted by permission of the author.

E. Ethelbert Miller, "The Voice of Aretha Franklin Surprises Me," *Carolina Quarterly* 50 (fall 1997). Copyright 1997. Reprinted by permission of the publisher.

Claude McKay, "If We Must Die." Courtesy of the Literary Representative for the Works of Claude McKay, Schomburg Center for Research in Black Culture, The New York Public Library, Astor, Lenox and Tilden Foundations.

"For My People," from Margaret Walker, *This Is My Century: New and Collected Poems* (Athens: University of Georgia Press, 1989). Copyright 1989. Reprinted by permission of the University of Georgia Press.

"Dear John, Dear Coltrane," from Michael S. Harper, *Songlines in Michaeltree: New and Collected Poems* (Champaign: University of Illinois Press, 2000). Copyright 2000 by Michael S. Harper. Used by permission of the poet and the University of Illinois Press.

"Revolutionary Music," from *Black Feeling, Black Talk, Black Judgment* (New York: William Morrow, 1968, 1970). Copyright © 1968, 1970 by Nikki Giovanni. Reprinted by permission of the poet and HarperCollins Publishers Inc. William Morrow.

Index

Abdul-Jabbar, Kareem (Lew Alcindor), 84–86, 88

Abdul-Khaalis, Hamaas, 85

Adderley, Julian "Cannonball," 60

Aesthetics: and cultural politics, 4, 82; black, 26–27, 31, 59, 69, 93, 95, 115; in visual art, 27, 108–110, 122, 129; physical aesthetics and beauty, 31, 34, 79, 96, 108, 110, 114, 127; in music, 59, 68, 73, 75, 134; in basketball, 82, 84, 92; in dance, 93–95, 97

Africa, Afrocentrism, 20–23, 31–33; and African liberation, 19, 33, 36, 62, 110; dual identity, 37–38, 40, 51; in music, 69, 72; in dance, 96; in visual art, 110, 114; in beauty, 114

African diaspora, 4, 21, 33, 37, 69, 71, 99, 137, 139

Agricultural Adjustment Administration (AAA), 12

Ailey, Alvin, 94, 95–98, 100; *Blues Suite,* 94; *Revelations,* 94

Albany Movement, 47–48

Ali, Muhammad (Cassius Clay), 41, 87, 88–91, 100

Alston, Charles, 27

Alvin Ailey American Dance Theatre, 93–98

Anderson, Queen C., 78

Andrews, Inez, 78

Anthropology, 29

Antiphony (call and response), 39, 66, 105, 134

Apartheid: in America, 53, 68; in South Africa, 137; opposition to, 137

Apollo Theater, 70

Appadurai, Arjun, 8

Armstrong, Louis, 57, 104, 105

Asian Americans, 20, 52; Filipino Americans, 134

Authenticity, 8, 34, 52, 70, 78, 119, 136

Baker, Ella, 7, 19

Baker, Houston A., Jr., 7

Balanchine, George, 97

Ballet, 95–98

Baraka, Imamu Amiri (LeRoi Jones), 6, 69; "In the Funk World," 69

Baseball, 83

Basie, Count, 57

Basketball: color line in, 83; ABA (American Basketball Association), 83–84; NBA (National Basketball Association), 83–84; and masculine urban cool, 84–86, 92

Bearden, Romare, 59, 102; *Conjur Woman, 103, 104; Of the Blues,* 103; *Projections, 107; Show Time, 104, 106*

Beatles, 79

Beatty, Talley, 94

Beauty. *See* Aesthetics

Berkeley: city of, 133; University of California at, 135, 136

Black Arts Movement, 83, 101, 116; and activism 6; and cultural nationalism, 28, 99; and Black Power, 115

Black Panther Party, 18, 19, 67, 114

Black Star, 139

Blakey, Art, 60

Blues, 2, 40, 46, 60–61, 63, 66, 72–73, 75, 77, 94, 103–104

Boogie-Woogie, 73, 75

Boxing, 83, 87, 89–90, 154

Boycotts, 7, 79; Montgomery bus boycott, 7, 15–16, 60, 79, 127; Olympic boycott (1968), 86–87

Brooks, Gwendolyn, 56

Brooks, Tina, 60

Brown, James, 67, 68–71, 133, 134; "Get Up, Get Into It and Get Involved," 70; "I Don't Want Nobody to Give Me Nothing," 70; "Say It Loud—I'm Black and I'm Proud," 70; "Talking Loud and Saying Nothing," 70

Brown, Sterling, 56

Brownlee, Archie, 78

Brown v. Board of Education (1954), 14–15, 16, 24, 59, 60, 127

Bruce, Lenny, 59

Caesar, Shirley (and the Caravans), "No Coward Soldier," 81

Caravans, The, "No Coward Soldier," 81

Carlos, John, 87

Carmichael, Stokely (Kwame Ture), 23, 25; *Black Power,* 23–24, 25

Carter, Robert L., 14, 15

Catlett, Elizabeth, 107–110, 114; *Black Is Beautiful,* 112, 114, *113*; *Homage to My Young Black Sisters,* 110, *111*; *Malcolm X Speaks for Us,* 112

Chamberlain, Wilt, 86

Chaney, James, 16

Charles, Ray, 67, 69; "Hit The Road Jack," 80

Cheeks, Reverend Julius, 80

Chicano Movement, 20

Christian exceptionalism, 120–121

Civil War, 76

Clark, Septima, 7

Clarke, Kenny, 58

Class, 3, 26, 31, 32, 97, 108, 116, 136, 138; as axis of identity, 26, 108, 116; white suburban middle class, 52, 136; classism, 108; working class, 125; as source of division, 136, 138

Cleaver, Eldridge, 90, 91

Clifford, James, 4

Clinton, George, 71–73

Coates, Dorothy Love, 80

Cold War, 15, 19, 109

Coleman, Ornette, 62–63

Coleman, Steve, 133

Coltrane, John, 62, 64–66, 85, 86, 129–130; "Alabama," 65; "Giant Steps," 85; "A Love Supreme," 66

Communism, 15–16, 19, 27–28

Congress of Industrial Organizations (CIO), 27

Congress of Racial Equality (CORE), 47

Cooke, Edna Gallmon, 78

Cooke, Sam, 68

Cosell, Howard, 87

Council of African Affairs, 19

Criminal justice: and police brutality, 13–14, 114; and incarceration, 48, 49, 71, 79, 89

Cuban Revolution, 19, 137

Cullen, Countee, 20; "Heritage," 20

Cultural nationalism, 6, 28, 97, 99, 114–115

Dance, 40, 54; moves and danceability, 40, 44–45, 61, 70, 79; and hard bop, 61; choreography, 70, 94–98; and funk, 72; and gospel, 78; concert, 93–94, 98; popular and social, 93, 95; ballet, 94, 95; modern, 94–98; break dancing, 134; and hip-hop, 134

Dance Theatre of Harlem, 93–94, 95–98

Davis, Francis, 64

Davis, Miles, 104, 105, 106

Davis, Thulani, 69

DeCarava, Roy, 99, 122–123, 124, 125–131; *Mississippi Freedom Marcher,* 127, *128*; *The Sweet Flypaper of Life* (with L. Hughes), 125–126

DeCarava, Sherry Turner, 129

Democratic National Convention (1964), 17

Denning, Michael, 27

Detroit Race Riot (1943), 13

Dolphy, Eric, 62

Double Victory Campaign, 13, 55

Douglas, Aaron, 27, 306

Du Bois, W. E. B., 4, 16, 19, 51

Dunham, Katherine, 94

Economics: economic stratification, 5, 12, 125; economic radicalism, 15; and affirmative action, 24; economic and job discrimination, 24, 30; economic stress, 27, 100; poverty, 30, 71, 87, 123; economic empowerment, 139. *See also* Class

Edwards, Brent, 41

Edwards, Harry, 86

Ellison, Ralph, 5, 27, 59

Erving, Julius (Dr. J), 83–84

Ethiopia, 19, 139

Europe, European-Americans, 47; colonialism, 19; WASPs, 35; European-American bias, 39, 99; Jews, 52; white ethnics, 52; European-American aesthetics, 93; Eurocentrism, 95–96, 97

Evans, Mari, 56

Evers, Medgar, 15

Executive Order 8802, 13

Fair Employment Practices Committee (FEPC), 13

Farm Security Administration (FSA), 123, 124, 126

Farmer, Art, 60

Feminism, 26, 108, 116

First World, 18, 20

Flack, Roberta, 131; "Be Real Black for Me," 131

Folklore, 14, 54, 56, 103

Folk practices, 119; and culture, 30, 95; and images, 103; and art, 119; music and storytelling, 119

Franklin, Aretha, 44–47, 49–50, 67–68, 79; "Call Me!," 46; "I Never Loved a Man (the Way I Loved You)," 46; "Respect," 67; "Share Your Love with Me," 46; "Spirit in the Dark," 46; "Think," 67; "To Be Young, Gifted, and Black," 80; "(You Make Me Feel Like) A Natural Woman," 46

Franklin, Dr. C. L., 67

Freedom rides, 7, 79

Funk, 69, 71–73, 79

Funkadelic, 71–72; "Free Your Mind and Your Ass Will Follow," 72

Galassi, Peter, 128–129

Garvey, Marcus, 30; Garveyism, 32, 55. *See also* Universal Negro Improvement Association

Gates, Henry Louis, Jr., 14

Gelburd, Gail, 103

Gender: as dimension of difference, 3, 26, 31–32, 50, 92n12, 108; sexuality, 26, 31, 32, 116; equality, 114; and visual artists, 116, 117, 119; stereotypes, 119; as point of fracture, 138

"Get Your Rights Jack," 80

Ghana, 18, 19

Gibson, Althea, 91

Gillespie, Dizzy, 57, 58

Ginsberg, Allen, 59

Giovanni, Nikki, 46–47, 67–68; "Poem for Aretha," 67; "Revolutionary Music," 68

Golden Gate Quartet, 80; "No Segregation in Heaven," 80

Goodman, Andrew, 16

Gospel, 45–46, 49, 60–61, 66, 67, 77–80

Great Britain, 19

Great Depression, 12, 15, 26, 30, 55, 61, 105, 122, 144n26

Great Repression, 15

Greensboro, N.C., 1

Guimond, James, 130

Gunn, Giles, 42

Hamer, Fannie Lou, 15, 16, 48, 49, 50

Hamilton, Charles V., *Black Power*, 23–24, 25

Harding, Vincent, 6, 7; and "fury for liberty," 7, 53

Harlem Art Workshop, 27

Harlem Renaissance (New Negro Renaissance), 20, 26, 27, 30, 32, 54, 55, 67, 98

Harper, Michael, 66; "Dear John, Dear Coltrane," 66

Harris, Norman, 54

Harris, R. H., 78

Hathaway, Donny, 131; "Be Real Black for Me," 131

Heilbut, Tony, 77, 78, 79, 80

Henderson, Harry, 110

Henderson, Stephen, 53–54

Hendrix, Jimmy, 71, 72–73; "Star Spangled Banner," 73

Henry, Aaron, 15

Herskovits, Melville J., 29

Herzog, Melanie Anne, 112

Hip-hop, 71, 132–139

Hochschild, Jennifer, 22
Horton, Lester, 95
Houston, Charles, 7, 14
Howard University School of Law, 14
Huggins, Nathan, xii, 42
Hughes, Langston, 27, 28, 30, 43, 56, 125–126; "I, Too, Sing America," 43; *The Sweet Flypaper of Life* (with Roy DeCarava), 125–126
Hurston, Zora Neale, 29, 30
Hybridity: and identity, 37, 39–41, 43, 65, 98; syncretic, 39–40, 94; in music, 40, 72–73, 79, 133

Impressions, The, 17, 68; "Keep on Pushin'," 68; "People Get Ready," 68; "This Is My Country," 17; "We're a Winner," 68
Improvisation: in jazz, 41, 63, 65–66, 73, 75; in sacred music, 80; in basketball, 83–84, 86; in boxing, 90; in visual art, 103, 129; in hip-hop, 133–134
Integration, 16, 23–25, 55, 61, 72, 98; in housing, 16; in schools, 16, 24, 100; and assimilation, 115
Intergalactic Arkestra (Sun Ra and His), 75
Invisibl Skratch Picklz, 133–134

Jackson, Mahalia, 78, 80; "Move On Up a Little Higher," 81
James, Etta, 67
Jazz, 2, 40, 45–46, 59, 66, 85–86, 104, 129–130; as metaphor, 41; and the Movement, 57–62; bebop, 58; hard bop and soul jazz, 60; jazz fusion, 61; free jazz, 61–75; swing, 61, 75; progressive jazz, 72; and hip-hop, 133–134
Jeffers, Lance, 10–11; "My Blackness Is the Beauty of This Land," 10–11
Jeter, Claude, 78
Jim Crow, 11, 23, 35, 55; collective action against, 1, 7; in the military, 13; legal fight against, 14, 15, 59; and equality, 53; in Washington, D.C., 123, 125
Johnson, Jack, 89

Jones, Charles, 47
Jones, Hank, 60

Kamoinge Workshop, 129
Karenga, Maulana Ron, 6
Kaufman, Bob, 59
Kelley, Robin D. G., 9, 28, 51
Kerouac, Jack, 59
King, Martin Luther, Jr., 7, 15, 16, 17, 19
Kouwenhoven, John A., 41
KPFA, 133
KRS-One, 139

Lange, Dorothea, 123
Larsen, Susan, 121
Latino Americans, 19, 20, 52
Lawrence, Jacob, 27, 99, 100–102, 105–106, 107, 108, 114, 115, 121; *Frederick Douglass* series (1938–39), 100; *Harriet Tubman* series (1939–40), 100; *The Migration of the Negro* series, 100; *The Ordeal of Alice, 101; Toussaint L'Ouverture* series (1937–38), 100
Levine, Lawrence, 23, 38
Lewis, David Levering, 69
Lewis, Samella, 116
"Lift Every Voice and Sing" (Negro National Anthem), 55
Lincoln, Abbey (Aminata Moseka), 62
Lincoln, Abraham, 17
Liston, Sonny, 88
Little Rock Nine, 100
Litweiler, John, 57, 63
Locke, Alain, 4
Lyons, Len, 63, 65

Macklin, Catherine, 33
Madhubuti, Haki R. (Don L. Lee), 56
Malcolm X, 16, 19, 85, 87, 88, 112
Malone, Jacqui, 92
Marches, 79, 132; led by A. Phillip Randolph (1941), 7, 12–13, 102; on Washington (1963), 17, 128; Poor People's March (1968), 79
Marcus, George E., 4

Marley, Bob (Robert Nesta), 139
Marshall, Thurgood, 14
Martin, Roberta, 78
May, Joe, 78
Mayfield, Curtis, 17, 68
McKay, Claude, 54, 55; "If We Must Die,"
54
McKayle, Donald, 94
Mercer, Kobena, 4
Migration, Great (First, Second), 12
Military, discrimination in, 13
Miller, E. Ethelbert, 46; "The Voice of
Aretha Franklin Surprises Me," 46
Mingus, Charles, 60, 62; "Prayer for Pas-
sive Resistance," 60; "Wednesday Night
Prayer Meeting," 60
Mississippi Freedom Summer, 16, 17
Mitchell, Arthur, 94–98; *Creole Giselle,* 97
Money, Mississippi, 15, 16
Monk, Thelonius, 58
Montgomery, Wes, 60
Montgomery bus boycott, 7, 15–16, 59–60,
79, 127
Morgan, Sister Gertrude, 99, 120–121; *The
Book of Revelation, 120*
Motown, 40, 71
Myrdal, Gunnar, *An American Dilemma,*
29

Natanson, Nicholas, 121, 125
Nation of Islam (Black Muslims), 85, 88
National Association for the Advance-
ment of Colored People (NAACP), 13,
14, 15
Native American movement, 20
Native Americans, 52
Neal, Larry, 6, 56
New Deal, 12
New World, 26, 32, 36, 37, 53, 91, 97. *See
also* African diaspora
New York City Ballet, 95
Nisenson, Eric, 64
"No Coward Soldier," 81

Olympics: 1968 boycott of, 86–87; 1960
boxing championship, 87

O'Meally, Robert G., 41
Organization of Black American Culture,
115
Orvell, Miles, 136

Pan-Africanism, 19, 21, 32–33, 37, 62, 71, 115;
roots of, 23, 25–26; repatriation, 25, 33;
African Commune of Bad Relevant
Artists (AFRI-COBRA), 115; *Wall of
Respect* (1967–71), 115; *Wall of Truth*
(1969), 115
Parker, Charlie "Bird," 57–59, 63, 65
Parks, Gordon, 122–125, 127, 130–131; *Ella
Watson, 124; Mrs. Ella Watson and Three
Grandchildren, 125, 126*
Patterson, Floyd, 88, 90–91
Patton, Sharon, 115
People of color: solidarity at home and
abroad, 18–20, 26; and identity, 21; as
outsiders, 51–52; women, 108, 112; youth,
133
Pickets, 49, 79
Plessy v. Ferguson (1896), 15
Pluralism, 119; and integration, 24–25, 98;
and activism, 109
Poetry, 30, 46, 54, 68; activist and political,
4, 56; jazz poetry, 41, 59, 66; poet philos-
ophers, 69; and visual art, 129; spoken
word poetry, 133
Poor People's March (1968), 7, 79
Pop music, 40, 58, 61
Popular Front, 27
Posnock, Ross, 4
Powell, Bud, 58
Presley, Elvis, 69
Protest. *See* Boycotts; Marches; Pickets;
Sit-ins; Teach-ins
Puerto Rican Independence, 19
Puerto Rican Movement, 52
Pynchon, Thomas, 59

Rainey, Gertrude "Ma," 104
Randolph, A. Philip, 12, 102
Reagon, Bernice Johnson, 79
Redding, Otis, 67
Reggae, 139

Revitalization: and community building, 14, 19, 21; and renewal, 27, 31–32, 68, 78; and assimilation, 38–40

Rhythm and blues, 2, 40, 61, 68, 72, 79

Ringgold, Faith, 116; *Slave Rape* series, 116; *Aunts Edith and Bessie* (*Family of Women* series), 116

Rivers, Larry, 59

Roach, Max, 58, 61, 64; "Freedom Now Suite," 61–62

Robeson, Paul, 7, 15, 19, 28, 37

Robinson, Jackie, 91

Rock Music, 61, 73, 79

Roosevelt, Eleanor, 12

Roosevelt, Franklin D., 12, 13

Rosenthal, David, 60

Russell, Bill, 86

Saar, Betye, 117–119; *Liberation of Aunt Jemima*, 117, *118*; *Spirit Catcher*, 117

Said, Edward, 7

Saint John Coltrane Will-I-Am African Orthodox Church, 64

Schwartzman, Myron, 107

Schwerner, Michael, 16

Selassie, Haile, 139

Self-determination: and autonomy, 3, 22, 28, 53, 70, 90, 110, 114; and self-imagining, 8, 27, 32, 35, 73, 88, 90, 115; and self-defense, 18, 67, 114; and Third World solidarity, 19, 26, 114; and pride, 24, 31, 34–36, 50–51, 54–56, 59, 84–85, 87, 90–91, 114, 136; and self-hatred, 32, 34–35, 51; and self-elevation, 57, 70

Separatism, 25, 33, 36–37, 88, 115, 134; nation within a nation, 36

Shahn, Ben, 123

Shepp, Archie, 64

Silver, Horace, 59

Simone, Nina, 68; "Four Women," 68; "I Wish I Knew How It Would Feel to Be Free," 76; "Mississippi Goddamn," 68

Sit-ins, 1, 7–9, 16, 62, 79

Sixteenth Street Baptist Church (Birmingham, Ala.), 65

Slavery, 4, 11, 35, 53, 76; resistance to, 17; postslavery, 30; and jazz commentary, 62

Sly and the Family Stone, 71, 72–73; "Stand," 71; "Thank You For Talkin' to Me Mother Africa," 71; "You Can Make It If You Try," 71

Smith, Bruce, 46; "Voice of Aretha in Italy," 47

Smith, Jimmy, 60

Smith, Tommie, 87

Song, 1–2, 17, 44–46, 50, 55–56, 58, 70, 73, 82, 105, 134, 137, 139; freedom songs, 45–46, 48–49, 78–81; and dance, 92–93

Soul music, 40, 46, 49–50, 61, 66–69, 72, 78, 79

Spirituals, 77, 79, 80, 95

Stepto, Robert, 54

Stryker, Roy, 123

Stuckey, Sterling, 37

Student Nonviolent Coordinating Committee (SNCC), 16, 48

Studio of Arts and Crafts, 27

Sun Ra (Herman Poole "Sonny" Blount), 62, 73–77

Swing music, 61, 73, 75

Szwed, John F., 58

Taylor, Dr. Billy, 76; "I Wish I Knew How It Would Feel to Be Free," 76

Taylor, Cecil, 62

Teach-ins, 132

Tennis, 91

306 Workshop, 27

Till, Emmet, 16

Toure, Askia Muhammad, 6, 68–69

Trachtenberg, Alan, 130

Truman, Harry, 15

Tucker, Ira, 78

Turner, Elizabeth M., 27

Universal Negro Improvement Association (UNIA), 30, 54

Urban/inner city, 31, 60, 74, 84, 85, 102, 136–138; insurrections, 18, 114; white suburban, 52, 136; urban North, 102–103

US Movement, 6

Van Deburg, William, 68, 87

Vernacular culture, 94; in oral art, 54; in music and folklore, 56; in poetry, 56, 60, 66; down home blues as, 60; blues and gospel as, 66; in dance, 92, 93, 95; in visual art, 100, 114

Vietnam war, 19, 26, 71, 89

Vincent, Ricky, 72

Visual art: paintings, 27, 41, 99–100, 102–103, 105, 114, 116, 120, 123, 130; murals and posters, 87, 96, 99, 103, 114–115, 127, 133; photography, 99, 103, 121–123, 125–130; collage, 102–103, 107, 138; sculpture, 108, 110; found art, 117–119; self-taught, 119–121

Waldron, Mal, 60

Walker, David, 37

Walker, Margaret, 55–56; "For My People," 55

Walton, Ortiz M., 59

Ward, Clara, 78

Washington, Booker T., 82

Watkins, Mel, 69

West, Cornel, 58, 68, 138

Williams, Marion, 78

Williams, Robert, 15

Women, 27, 68, 87, 97, 103, 108, 110, 114; violence against, 13–14, 115–116; white, 16, 123; as cultural caretakers, 50; as people of color, 52, 108, 112; conjure women, 103; blueswomen, 104–105; as agents of unity, 105; feminist, 107, 116; young, 110, 112, 128; as mothers, 112; in AFRI-COBRA, 115; as Jemima, 117; charwomen, 123

Women's Army Corps (WAC), 13–14

Wood, Grant, 123; "American Gothic," 123

World War I, 54, 74

World War II, 1, 12–13, 15, 19 29–30, 55, 73–74, 125

Youth activism, 1, 16, 22, 48, 86, 100, 112, 128, 136–137; antiwar, 132–133

Zinn, Howard, 49